Plant Your Money Tree

Plant Your Money Tree

A Guide to Growing Your Wealth

Michele Schneider

Rowman & Littlefield
Lanham • Boulder • New York • London

Published by Rowman & Littlefield
An imprint of The Rowman & Littlefield Publishing Group, Inc.
4501 Forbes Boulevard, Suite 200, Lanham, Maryland 20706
www.rowman.com

6 Tinworth Street, London SE11 5AL, United Kingdom

Distributed by NATIONAL BOOK NETWORK

British Library Cataloguing in Publication Information Available

Library of Congress Cataloging-in-Publication Data

Names: Schneider, Michele, 1954– author.
Title: Plant your money tree : a guide to growing your wealth / Michele
    Schneider.
Description: Lanham : Rowman & Littlefield, [2019] | Includes index.
Identifiers: LCCN 2018047265 (print) | LCCN 2018048083 (ebook) | ISBN
    9781538122587 (electronic) | ISBN 9781538122570 (pbk. : alk. paper)
Subjects: LCSH: Finance, Personal. | Wealth.
Classification: LCC HG179 (ebook) | LCC HG179 .S294 2019 (print) | DDC
    332.024/01—dc23
LC record available at https://lccn.loc.gov/2018047265

∞™ The paper used in this publication meets the minimum requirements of
American National Standard for Information Sciences—Permanence of Paper
for Printed Library Materials, ANSI/NISO Z39.48-1992.

Printed in the United States of America

I dedicate this book to everyone who wishes to rise above the media fray and differing opinions of the analysts and talking heads and, instead, desires to learn how to drive their own financial success.

CONTENTS

FIGURES

INTRODUCTION

This book fulfills a dream. As a financial trader and teacher, I want to give every person the ability to successfully navigate through what many believe is beyond their comprehension: the economy. And not just the economy—specifically, the job, real estate, and stock markets. Let's face it, whether we want to deal with it or not, the economy rules so many aspects of our lives that it is unavoidable. This book empowers you by giving you the tools to make independent, informed decisions about your and your family's financial life.

Do you wonder what to do with your money? Do you wonder how to get more money? Are you confused about making personal choices such as changing careers, guiding your kid's education, expanding your business, buying a house, putting your money in the bank, deciphering social trends, and investing in the future?

Do you know who is managing your 401(k)? Do you think it doesn't really matter who is controlling your money? After all, brokers and financial planners are all the same anyway. How many of you do not have a 401(k) but would like to make some investments for your family's future, yet are afraid to make a mistake? If you want to learn more about the workings of the market, aspects of the economy, and how they impact you and your 401(k) but have felt too uninformed or confused to get it, this book is for you.

1

As an introduction of what you will learn in this book, let me give you a brief tour of what is to come. While this all may seem confusing to you now, stay with me, and you will easily understand how market phases can play a very important role in your life!

I started this book in January 2015, when the people's perspectives were bullish (meaning that the stock market was rising). Midway through September 2015, nearly everything turned bearish (the stock market was falling). By the time I came close to concluding the book, the phases had gone through a full cycle and then some. In the late winter/early spring of 2016, most of the sectors returned to the Bullish Phase. Then, by the fall of 2016, certain sectors returned to the Caution Phase (stock market prices declined from their highest levels). In 2017, the U.S. stock market hit new all-time highs. In late 2018, another new all-time high was reached, followed by a substantial sell-off. This book has evolved through the phases not as theory, but as a living entity. Market phases help to describe an instrument's strength or weakness. Financial instruments such as the Dow Jones Industrial Average move from one phase to another, based on Moving Averages.

In a period of three years, the global economy and the markets have reflected optimism as well as doom and gloom. Some economists have predicted recession (a decline in gross domestic product [GDP] for two or more consecutive quarters), while others see continued growth. We have seen certain megatrends (such as online shopping) explode, while other megatrends (like 3-D printing) lag. Megatrends are global, sustained, and macroeconomic forces of development that affect business, the economy, society, cultures, and personal lives, thereby defining our future world and its increasing pace of change. Many of the examples I analyze and illustrate are from 2008–2016. Those eight years may be historic; however, the information gleaned from these examples is evergreen! One must understand the past to predict the future.

Through it all, boom or bust, predictions of extremes have been amplified by social media and 24-hour news loops. It's enough to make the savviest investor's head spin. Even in the best of times, the understanding of how and why sectors of the economy, commodities, and the stock market cycle from boom to bust eludes most people. If you are like so many others counting on central banks to show you the way, the fact is that they have some real issues they cannot figure out for themselves. Central banks, such as the Federal Reserve and its branches, are national banks that uniquely control money, credit, monetary policy, and the regulation of member banks.

While the public licked its wounds after the fallout of 2008, financial planners suffered from posttraumatic stress, and the media continually reported on the horrible state of affairs, I encouraged our followers to buy when the stock indices were near their lows. All it took to give me the confidence to make such a bold recommendation was one very simple indicator—the 50-week Moving Average (50-WMA).

So, why read this book? Maybe if you had a compass or a navigation system that you could easily comprehend, you would consider investing. The good news is that without a barrier to entry, it's easy for anyone to get started in investing. So even if you never wish to make an investment, you can still research and empower yourself with knowledge about anything you need to know that has a direct impact on your life, your job, your kid's education, home buying, refinancing, and loan decisions.

With a master's degree in special education, and as a highly successful commodities (raw materials or primary agricultural products, bought and sold, such as copper or coffee) and stock market trader, I combine a lifetime of knowledge to bring you this "all-inclusive" book on the phases of the economy and the stock market.

I have three passions in life: trading, teaching, and writing. For this book, I called upon all three passions to come up with a way to help you, the reader, have a deeper understanding of the trends or phases in the market. I consider this book a "modified" curriculum of the economy and the effect it has on your life. Its intention is to allow anyone and everyone "access" to the curriculum in a salient and empowering way.

Reading this book will help you learn about a simple, yet powerfully accurate way to look at your financial life with a completely new attitude of confidence. This is not "The Secret." You only manifest what you want with work and knowledge. It requires some thinking on your part, of course, but I will stay with you every step of the way.

A great honor and distinction: In December 2016, *MarketWatch*, an online publication owned by Dow Jones, published "The Twitter Accounts Investors Need to Follow." Written by Barbara Kollmeyer, her subtitle read, "These Financial Tweeters Will Make You Money or at Least Make You Laugh." She goes on to write,

> It's that time again. That is, time for you to clean out your Twitter closet. . . . Toss the bots and Eggheads, and add a few names who might actually give good guidance in what is sure to be an interesting year for investors. Michele Schneider, Director of research and trading education at MarketGauge, tosses up techs and charts.

Ms. Kollmeyer honors me with the distinction of including me on that list! Thank you, Ms. Kollmeyer. I will try to make you and my readers proud (and profitable)!

Come with me, and I promise you will lose your intimidation toward money and exponentially gain confidence as a consumer and investor.

CHAPTER ONE

THE BEAUTY OF PHASES

W ould you like to make your financial decisions with a new level of consistency and certainty? What if you no longer had to rely on the talking heads, analysts, financial planners, or your smart next-door neighbor to help you decide when to buy a house, borrow money, change career paths, or get involved in the stock market?

If you are like me, living in a world that moves so randomly that all of the conflicting information flying at us with blinding speed further confuses you, then you seek simplicity and certainty.

Yes, the market is complex. Yet I have spent more than thirty-five years studying both big (macro) and small (micro) trends. The six phases of the market have successfully guided me and, by extension, the thousands of folks I have taught and continue to teach during seminars and webinars, as well as through e-books, my daily blog, and social media. The six phases are as follows: Bullish, Caution, Distribution, Bearish, Recuperation, and Accumulation. I will cover how to identify and use each phase to make money decisions fully in ensuing chapters.

Another way to think about these phases is to see them as six pictures that tell six stories and evoke six different emotions. Each of these six stories/emotions influences every aspect of your life. How

5

money flows directly and indirectly affects us all. The six stories help you identify changes you need to make, when to make them, and how to proceed. Once you identify the time to make a change, each story sets you up with specific guidelines to follow. These guidelines give you the knowledge and the autonomy to make intelligent decisions that could make your and your family's lives a lot better!

Phases in the market cycle occur as inherently as they do in nature. If you know what the phase or cycle is, you have a road map for what to do. We all know that you don't plant when the ground is frozen. Depending upon where they live, most people plant sometime after Mother's Day. This is a guideline of nature.

The same is true with the inherent nature of market phases. If you know which phase the market, any sector of the economy, or the stock of the company you work for is in, you will know when to put money in the bank or stuff it under a mattress. You will know the best time to buy a house and which field of study has potential for your kids to pursue as a career. You will know when to invest (or not). You will understand what your IRA and 401(k) accounts are doing and why. That's the simple power of reading and interpreting these six stories I am calling "phases."

The concept of phases and Moving Averages is not new. Charles Dow, cofounder of Dow Jones & Company and founder of the *Wall Street Journal*, also invented the Dow Jones Industrial Average (DJIA). He laid the groundwork for technical analysis and was the first to talk about phases. Dow used four: Accumulation, Public Participation, Distribution, and Panic. Richard D. Wyckoff, in 1931, developed the Wyckoff Method, which uses four phases making up cycles for stocks: Accumulation, Markup, Distribution, and Markdown. In 1937, during the Great Depression, Sir John Templeton (known as one of the top stock pickers of all time) pegged four different phases: Pessimism, Skepticism, Optimism, and Euphoria. In 1988, Stan Weinstein wrote his *Secrets for Profiting in Bull and Bear Markets*.[1] Weinstein uses "Stages": Basing (similar to our Recuperation Phase), Advancing (like the Accumulation Phase), Top Area

6

(similar to our Caution Phase), and Declining (like Distribution), Weinstein uses a 30-week Moving Average for long-term investing. This book widens the time period out to 50- and 200-week Moving Averages (50- and 200-WMAs) for investing and other money decisions.

More recently, Laszlo Birinyi, an investment professional, identified four phases: Reluctance, Digestion, Acceptance, and Exuberance. Chuck Dukas, in *The TRENDadvisor Guide to Breakthrough Profits: A Proven System for Building Wealth in the Financial Markets*,[2] writes about six market phases: Bullish, Warning, Distribution, Bearish, Recovery, and Accumulation. Dukas likewise employs the 50- and 200-period Moving Averages. Many other traders have used the 50- and the 200-day Simple Moving Averages to make trading and investing decisions. For example, William O'Neil, founder of *Investor's Business Daily* and author of *How to Make Money Selling Stocks Short*,[3] chiefly uses the 50- and 200-day and -week Moving Averages to determine how poorly or strongly a company's stock is behaving.

Compiling from the masters, I take the concept of phases and Moving Averages to another level. As each of these mentors talks about phases referring to stocks and the financial markets, I show you how to use the phase's road map to gauge how and when to make *all* money decisions. I point out six specific instruments that represent the most salient features of the U.S. economy and show you how to identify each phase, which helps you make informed money decisions. Furthermore, I identify the corresponding human emotions tied to each cycle or phase.

How do you identify a phase? We all learned how to read a bar chart in school. This process is no different, except it comes with the sensibility of a special education teacher. I rehash the same elementary school lessons you learned about reading bar charts and show you how to apply this knowledge to making sound financial decisions. Reading bar charts is just like reading a compass. A compass has two needles. We all know how to look at those two needles on a compass to see which way is north, south, east, and west. All the bar charts I illustrate have two lines. Like a compass, those two lines will help you identify the direction, cycle, and/or phase of the economy. Those lines will serve as your compass so you always know when to make the most appropriate financial decisions.

Identifying the phase of six different bar charts will give you all the information you need. You will have as much, if not more, expertise about making financial decisions as the professional analysts and fund managers have. No more disconnect because of a lack of understanding that leads to fear. Fear is a result of confusion. If you prepare for the bad and the good phases, there is no need for fear. Being prepared to cut back or push forward as needed because you can read the phases yourself is empowering on so many levels. Regardless of your income level, it's easier to improve your life when you can make educated decisions.

I am a special-education-teacher-turned-trader who still teaches. I manage money and trade recommendations in a state of calm because I know what's before me and what that implies for the future. I can't control what happens, but I can and do control my attitude about what is and what will be. I make *all* my financial decisions based on these six stories.

In this book, I illustrate the simplest way for you to do the same. It begins by first identifying which of the six phases any aspect of the economy, the market, or a company is in at that moment. The formula is as easy as reading two lines on a chart.

CHAPTER TWO
MOVING AVERAGES—
A UNIVERSAL LANGUAGE

Everything you need to learn to take you from a state of confusion to a state of empowerment begins with two basic concepts: Moving Averages and phases.

What's So Important about Averages?

Try going a day without some thought about an average. Average calories you should eat per day; average temperature for the month in your town or the place you want to go to visit. Or, for you baseball aficionados, how about batting averages? Have you thought recently about the average life span of a man versus a woman? Perhaps the average life span of different breeds of dogs might influence which breed you will adopt. Have you ever tried to buy anything on credit? That's right, you are financially judged on your average credit score. Do you have a child about to go to college? If so, I'll bet you are thinking about the average SAT score that he or she will need before applying to schools.

Merriam-Webster's Dictionary defines an average as "the sum of a list of numbers divided by the number of numbers in the list; a number expressing the central or typical value in a set of data."

The basic premise of this chapter is to familiarize you with Moving Averages. Given a time series, such as daily stock market prices or yearly temperatures, people often want to create a smoother series.[1] This helps show underlying trends or perhaps periodic behavior. These mathematically based averages have a statistically high probability of taking lagging data to predict future movement.

Before I cover the basic and simple premise of Moving Averages, I'd like to tell you a little bit about Newton's laws of motion, railway engineering, and how simple physics is a concept we all know intimately because we live with it every day, and it impacts everything we have come to take for granted. Nothing I cover in this chapter is new to anyone. We all learned about Newton's laws in our early grades in school. Some of us might have been paying closer attention; therefore, I dedicate this chapter to those who may have snoozed through physics classes thinking, "What does any of this have to do with my life?"

The truth is that the simple concepts of physics work their way into our lives in multiple ways. The creation of the internet is largely due to physics. Without physics, there would be no smartphones, laptops, microwave popcorn, beer foam, architecture, mining, and fuel consumption—hence, nothing to power planes, trains, and automobiles.

I am not suggesting we need to become physicists to grasp the concept of Moving Averages and phases; yet it is important that you accept simple physics as the cornerstone of understanding Moving Averages. From there, we have the necessary framework to identify all of the market phases. After all, isn't it comforting to know that what I am offering you in its simplest form is based on math and science that goes back hundreds (if not thousands) of years? Would you want to put your faith is something that has not been proven over time?

Laws of Motion

Sir Isaac Newton (1643–1727), an English physicist and mathematician, formulated three basic ideas about motion—his three laws of motion. Newton's laws are very important because they tie into almost *everything* we see in everyday life. A perfect example is driving a car. In order for a car to move, there must be friction between the wheels and the ground. The wheels exert a force on the ground because they are spinning, and the ground creates a reaction force on the wheels. This force pushes the car forward. So thank Newton's law of action and reaction every time you drive!

Newton's first law states that an object at rest tends to stay at rest, and an object in motion tends to stay in motion. If there is a lack of motion, nothing will change until something or someone applies force to engender motion. Furthermore, Newton gathered that once one applies the necessary force to put something into motion, that something will move in that specific direction until another, stronger force stops that motion.

This theory also applies to Moving Averages and the movement of prices in the stock market. A stock that doesn't move up or down very much will stay at rest until something compels it to move. For instance, if an analyst says to buy or sell a stock because the company's earnings are far beyond or below expectations or the company is being bought by another company, these factors can become the "force" that puts the stock in motion.

Newton's second law says that the acceleration of an object relates to the applied force or magnitude of the force, and there will be different accelerations (changes in motion) depending upon the size or mass of that object. This is a pertinent law for physics but has little to do with our purposes in describing Moving Averages.

The third law states that for every action (force), there is an equal and opposite reaction (force). This is easy to picture; when air rushes out of a balloon, the opposite reaction is that the balloon flies up.

The third law relates to an event that could have an opposite and equal force on the market's action. For instance, war breaking out could act as the balloon mentioned here. Hence, if the reaction is to force the market into fear, the action will be that the market participants rush out of the market. With a Moving Average, the reaction to a watershed event may force the price to test, surge through, or break down from that Moving Average.

Trains and Moving Averages

Fascination with trains has never been my thing, aside from dreaming about a romantic train ride through a cityscape such as the one depicted in the 1983 film *Risky Business*, starring Tom Cruise. For me, that was the best scene in the film. Through photography, music, and editing, the director created an almost abstract world.

My purpose here is to take what many may perceive as an abstract concept and reshape it into something concrete and incredibly easy to use. After all my years in the investment business, I've concluded that the simplest way to empower someone in making objective, informed, and sound decisions about most financial concerns is to look at two Simple Moving Averages (SMA). A Simple Moving Average is the average of a stock's closing prices (minute, hour, day, week, or month) over a certain period. The shorter-term SMAs are faster to respond to market action than the longer-term SMAs. For this book, I primarily use 50- and 200-week Moving Averages (50- and 200-WMAs).

Using trains to explore simple physics will make Moving Averages concrete, sexy, and, well, something we all can pleasurably and easily imagine.

Two concepts to consider regarding trains and physics:

1. If an object is moving, it has momentum (speed); consequently, increasing mass, velocity, or both increases momentum.

2. Trains vary in mass; mass coupled with the direction and angle of the slope the train is traveling on will determine whether it will pick up or lose momentum.

A freight train is typically massive. When you see one moving along the tracks parallel to your car as you drive, compared to the speed you are traveling, it looks like the train is barely moving. But that train has built up momentum so it *can* keep moving. As the engine (front of the train) starts moving, it pulls on the first car *before* it feels the weight of the third car or any behind it. This gives the engine its own momentum plus that of the second car to begin pulling the third. This continues down the length of the train, using the constantly increasing overall momentum until all of the cars are moving.

Now imagine two trains moving—one with 200 cars, and the other with 50 cars. If momentum is a measure of mass in motion, then a 200-car freight train will have a different speed from one with 50 cars. Why? Because momentum equals mass times velocity.[2]

If scientists calculate momentum by multiplying the mass of an object by the velocity of the object, it provides an indication of how hard it would be to stop the object. The longer the freight train, the longer it takes to stop. Therefore, an engineer of an Amtrak train applies the brakes long before the train arrives at the station to ensure the train will come to a halt at the station, while the engineer of a small-scale train at an amusement park applies brakes just moments before entering the station.

Do you remember Newton's first law of physics? It said that without interference, any object moving would continue moving. That idea applies to momentum as well. The momentum of an object will never change if left alone.

What Do Trains, Sir Isaac Newton, Mass, Momentum, and Speeds (Velocity) Have to Do with Moving Averages?

A Moving Average is the most widely used indicator (datasets that use statistical formulas that tell you about the health of different markets, groups, and related stocks). Moving Averages smooth out price action over time, and by taking the average closing price for the last 50- or 200-week periods, you can more readily identify a trend or phase. From past price action, it becomes more statistically viable to forecast future price action.

Before I go any further, the term *technical analysis* refers to multiple methodologies for forecasting the direction of prices through the study of past market data, primarily price and volume. Like weather forecasting, technical analysis does not result in absolute predictions about the future. Instead, technical analysis can help investors anticipate what is "likely" to happen to prices over time.

Forecasting direction is naturally open to interpretation. Experienced investors who use technical analysis will use a variety of indicators in addition to Moving Averages. For our purposes, I have found that *simple* is not only better for a novice but also the easiest way to understand how one makes predictions. The constant blast of information available goes beyond overkill. Then add interpretations or "opinions" and it leaves you feeling numb, confused, and alienated.

Although we begin here with two Simple Moving Averages, we will easily move toward the ability to determine the phase of any instrument or economic trend because of what those Moving Averages are telling us. I will also highlight where both the best and the worst decisions were made during all phases based on actual events of the recent past.

You will be able to "see" for yourself that you can determine what actions you should or should not take to protect and/or invest your money at any point of an economic cycle (since you will know what the "experts" know). With this knowledge, you will finally have the independent ability to make decisions on the best or worst times to put your money in the bank, pay off or take out a loan, buy a house or car, invest in the stock market, or just exponentially reduce worry, fear, and anxiety about investing and financial literacy.

How to Read a Chart

Throughout the book, I use charts frequently. Most of the charts used for illustration purposes in this book come from TradeStation, the platform or trading software we use at MarketGauge.

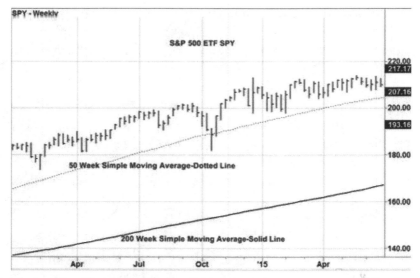

Figure 2.1. The S&P 500 April 2014–May 2015 (Courtesy of Trade-Station Technologies, Inc.)

On the top line of figure 2.1, starting from left to right, is the symbol or name of the instrument. In this case, SPY is the Standard and Poor's 500 ETF, which is an index of the largest Fortune 500 companies. Each bar represents the price for a full week. The bar chart shows a high and low and a dash that represents the closing price for the week. The right side (or the vertical axis) shows the price points, and the bottom (horizontal axis) tells you the dates. The dotted line represents the 50 simple Weekly Moving Average and the solid line the 200 simple Weekly Moving Average.

Moving Averages

The Moving Average (MA) may be the most universal of all technical analysis indicators. Initially, the only type of Moving Average used was a simple arithmetic average because it was easy to understand and quick to calculate. This made it a standout in a world of technical analysis that predated computers.

15

A Moving Average simplifies price data by smoothing it out and creating one flowing line. This can make isolating trends easier. Common Moving Average lengths are 10, 20, 50, 100, and 200. The period of time you choose for a Moving Average, also called the "look back period," can play a big role in how effective it is.

An MA with a short time frame will react much more quickly to price changes than an MA with a longer look-back period. For this book, I will illustrate a weekly chart. The weekly chart will use 50- and 200-week SMAs.

On a weekly chart, a 50-week SMA adds the closing price of each week and then divides it by 50. The 200-week SMA adds the closing price of each week and then divides it by 200. The 200-week Moving Average (200-WMA) may be the granddaddy of Moving Averages. Simply put, a financial instrument that is trading above it is healthy; one below it is anemic. The 200-WMA measures the sentiment of the market on a longer-term basis. This is where major players like pension plans and hedge funds need to look in order to move a large amount of stocks.

Since so many traders and investors watch the 200-WMA, once a price point reaches, fails, or holds it, the collective psychology creates an immediate impact. Additionally, the longer Moving Average takes into account the prime movers of the markets and prices.

These two (50- and 200-WMAs) are commonly used by institutional investors. When the 200-WMA (or close to four years) is positive, typically it means investors are buying the market. And vice versa. The 50-WMA measures the price trend for about one year's time. By identifying a current price of any instrument and how it stacks up against these two MAs, you can a identify phase, which gives you invaluable information.

Earlier I mentioned that if you imagine two trains moving—one with 200 cars, the other with 50 cars—the momentum (or mass times velocity) of a 200-car freight train would be different from a 50-car train's. For active investors—those who tend to move money in and out of the market faster—the MAs used most often to determine the market's intermediate to long-term trend, respectively, are the 50 and 200 Daily Moving Averages (DMAs). As we are looking further out than the typical active investor is, Weekly Moving Averages (WMAs) work best for long-term investments and life-altering decisions.

A train with 200 cars takes longer to get up to speed, and once it's in motion, it will stay in motion longer. Comparing that to a 200-WMA, once a price clears the 200-WMA, the trend will remain in one direction for a longer period; even if price fluctuates, the 200-WMA tunes out the "noise."

Furthermore, if we recall Newton and his laws of motion (simple physics), changing this situation requires an external force to act. In the case of the 200-WMA with the price going from above it to below it, this external force means that some indicators or events have the power to change the trend of the stock market. It may be some economical factor, some news, a political event, a trend in foreign exchange, or even the collective psychology of the market that can change the ongoing trend of the stock.

Like a freight train leading 200 cars, it takes a lot of braking to stop the price movement—an opposing and equal force—and that reversal takes considerable time, giving investors ample time to adjust their investment strategy.

Can You Identify Emerging Trends in a Timely Fashion?

For example, 2007–2008 was a tough time for the Real Estate sector. As an introduction to the effectiveness of having the 50 and 200 simple Weekly Moving Averages with no other tools at your disposal, figure 2.2 illustrates how you would have had the information and been prepared well in advance of the real estate bubble. Some of my favorite indicators to watch for emerging trends in the stock market indices and for the major sectors of the economy that impact us all on a daily basis are exchange-traded funds (ETFs). Simply put,

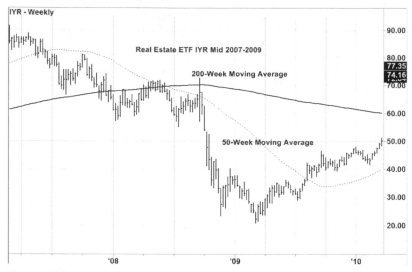

Figure 2.2. Real Estate ETF (IYR) February 2007–February 2010 (Courtesy of TradeStation Technologies, Inc.)

ETFs are pooled investment vehicles that allow investors to buy or sell a basket of companies' stocks or a blend of assets in commodities, bonds, stocks, or currencies. I like ETFs, as they give investors a way to diversify among many instruments within a specific sector of the market. Unlike mutual funds, an ETF trades like a common stock on a stock exchange throughout the day. ETFs experience price changes throughout the day as they trade. Mutual funds, by contrast, are a professionally managed investment fund collected from many investors for investing in stocks, bonds, or money markets that match a stated investment objective. Mutual funds only trade once per day.

In fact, during the course of this book, I will highlight mainly ETFs to represent all areas of the U.S. and global economies. The chart in figure 2.2 is iShares Dow Jones U.S. Real Estate Index Fund Ticker symbol: IYR Investment type: ETF, listed on the New York Stock Exchange. The iShares Dow Jones Real Estate Index

Fund measures the performance of companies associated with the real estate industry.

A stock *index* or stock market *index* is a measurement of the value of a group of stocks incorporated in that index. Once you can identify each of the six phases (or six market cycles), you will better understand that IYR phases deteriorated quickly. From mid-2007, when IYR entered a Caution Phase, until mid-2009, when it crossed from Bearish into a Recuperation Phase, the price fell from ninety dollars to nearly twenty dollars!

Hindsight being 20/20, you could look at the bar chart and think, "Oh, if only I knew that in 2007, I would have tried to sell my house, refinanced before the prices depreciated, or not bought another house."

And for those who do invest, you might have considered checking out your real estate holdings and exiting or selling short (when you sell an ETF anticipating it will go lower) the Real Estate ETF (IYR).

In fact, one of the top headlines from 2007 came from Goldman Sachs, now infamously known as one of the last Wall Street giants to enter the lucrative world of subprime mortgages. However, it wasn't long before the elite investment house was cutting deals with high-flying firms, such as California's New Century Financial, whose lax standards would prove disastrous. Perhaps no lender was more emblematic of the subprime mortgage industry's spectacular rise and fall.

Goldman Secretly Bet on the U.S. Housing Crash

In 2006 and 2007, Goldman Sachs Group allegedly peddled more than $40 billion in securities backed by at least 200,000 risky home mortgages, but they never told the buyers they were secretly betting that a sharp drop in U.S. housing prices would send the value of those securities plummeting.

I watch ETFs as the best and easiest ways to track where your money should and should not go. Remember, I am not advocating that you all become traders or active investors. I am emphasizing that you can learn to read the current and emerging trends in these critical areas of the economy that affect everyone, and once you do learn this, you will have the knowledge and the power to make objective and informed decisions with very little risk.

Watching the two Simple Moving Averages and seeing how they relay the phase of the instrument told me everything I needed to know about the instrument in question to move forward and help guide investors through the huge impending crash of 2008.

To review, calculate a Moving Average by averaging price values from a specified number of bars. Specifically, there are two parameters (inputs) for a Moving Average formula:

- Price—a single price value from each bar used in calculating the average; traditionally, the price value used is the closing price of each bar.

- Length—the specified number of bars, counting backward from the current, or the most recent bar from which to draw the data points.

The "moving" part of a Moving Average is not actually in any of the formulas. As each new bar is built, the oldest data point is dropped from the series (or its impact is reduced) and the price value from the new bar is added to the series.

Summary

1. Moving Averages comprise time series data over consecutive periods. These are natural extensions of simple physics using mass, momentum, and speed.

2. The 50- and 200-day Simple Moving Averages evaluate price going back 50 and 200 days, respectively, and are widely considered the two most reliable indicators for active investing. If you are a longer-term investor or want to make life-changing decisions, the 50 and 200 simple WMAs work reliably.

3. Using the relation of these two Moving Averages to one another is the basis of identifying the phase of any instrument on a daily or a weekly chart.

4. After you determine the phase (cycle), you will have more information than most traders and "experts."

CHAPTER THREE
THE BIG 6

T he best way to read the chart in figure 3.1 is clockwise. It illustrates how I will enumerate the chapters, beginning with the Bullish Phase, or what I like to call "High Noon."

Phase in *Merriam-Webster's Dictionary* is defined as follows: "A distinct period or stage in a process of change or forming part of something's development."

Synonyms: stage, period, chapter, episode, part, step, point, time, and juncture.

The same method applies to economic and stock trends. Understanding the "distinct periods" of change when financial trends begin and end will empower you. Knowing about phases will help you "see" the different stages of a trend clearly.

There Are Six Phases

The chart in figure 3.1 illustrates the flow of the six phases in the market. Most people are familiar with the terms "bullish" and "bearish." If you look at the chart like time on a clock, beginning with the Bullish Phase as high noon, you can see that, moving clockwise, certain factors (whether they be economic, geopolitical, or even psychological) might spook the market, moving it into the next phase:

Market Phases

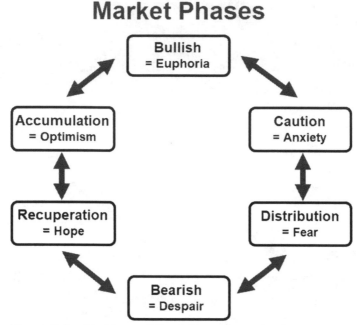

Figure 3.1. Six Phases Wheel (chart by author)

Caution. From there, if factors should become more negative, the phase will deteriorate into a Distribution Phase. If things deteriorate even further, there could be a decline into a Bearish Phase.

Recognizing Phases Is Like Having GPS

Knowing the market phases and what course of action to take in any given phase—whether it's to gauge the overall market, a sector of the economy, or an individual stock—is like having your own GPS. With GPS, you know where you are starting from and what direction you need to go in so you never feel or get lost.

The beauty of independently identifying and evaluating typical characteristics is in preparing for and taking action on each phase, which allows you to stay in step long before the news confirms the reason why a phase changes.

Most technical analysts (chartists) will tell you that the chart precedes the news. Imagine having the time to prepare for a downturn in advance rather than waiting for some "expert" to tell you that things are worsening. Or, in the opposite scenario, picture having a jump start on investing or making good financial decisions before the experts tell you to buy!

Perhaps the best feature of understanding phases is that like everything in life, there are cycles. Eventually, everything moves through each cycle. Often, a financial instrument might move in between two cycles, going back and forth for a long time before finding momentum in one phase or the other. In investments terms, momentum refers to the rate of change on price movements for a particular asset—that is, the speed at which the price is changing. The comforting part is that with the knowledge of phases you will gain from this book, you will be able to pinpoint when the conditions and phases improve.

Real Estate—A Trip Back to 2007

Going back to the example of the Real Estate Sector (IYR), well before the 2008 crash there were early signs when the phase deteriorated from Bullish to Caution. That Caution predicted the 2008 crash. Furthermore, in April 2009, the worst was over when the phase improved from a Bear Phase to a Recuperation Phase.

In 2009, the Real Estate ETF bottomed out, and by the end of March and beginning of April, the phase turned more positive, to a Recuperation Phase. This was a strong signal, as the 50-week Moving Average (50-WMA) also began to flatten, eventually sloping upward.

Perhaps some of you were following, but if you weren't, that turned out to be the *bottom* of the Real Estate meltdown and the bottom of the stock market for the next nine years! Were the pundits telling you that? Was your financial planner helping you scope out cheap real estate deals? Were most of you prepared at all for perhaps the best opportunity in the real estate sector in this century?

Perhaps you saw this headline:

U.S. Commercial Property Market Thawing

(Reuters)—The gap between U.S. commercial property buyers and sellers is narrowing, indicating the shattered market is closer to beginning the painful path to recovery, said the head of Prudential Real Estate Investors.

Would you have believed this useful news story given that most financial planners and money market managers were in the throes of posttraumatic stress disorder?

You might have if you had looked at the Real Estate ETF chart in figure 3.1 and could independently recognize the phase change to Recuperation. As you will learn, given the parameters of how weak or strong a phase change is, this one indicated strength.

Several months prior, a headline read, "Markets in Disarray as Lending Locks Up."[1]

Had you looked at the weekly chart of the S&P 500 in the beginning of 2008 and saw the phase change to Bearish, you would have been well ahead of the headlines seen all over the world in September 2008.

Throughout this book, I refer to the U.S. stock market and the top economic sectors and groups. When referencing the overall U.S. stock market, I am mainly referring to the S&P 500. The S&P 500 is short for the Standard and Poor's 500. Market analysts use the S&P commonly as a representation for the total stock market.

Depending on headlines from analysts and investors engendered even more confusion. By April 2009, headlines were reading, "Why the Economy Is Showing Green Shoots."[2]

Warren Buffet was making headlines as well. As he said to CNBC, "U.S. Economy in 'Shambles.' No Signs of Recovery Yet."[3]

Posttraumatic Stress Impacts 93 Percent of Financial Advisors

The professionals were equally and stunningly confused. Nearly every single financial professional interviewed reported medium to high levels of posttraumatic stress, according to a study published in the *Journal of Financial Therapy*. The survey—"Financial Trauma: Why the Abandonment of Buy-and-Hold in Favor of Tactical Asset Management May Be a Symptom of Post-Traumatic Stress"—found that another 40 percent of planners reported severe symptoms. The respondents managed assets with an average value of between $20 million and $40 million.[4] So, how can we, the little guys, possibly know where to turn and what to do?

Easy: the phases!

According to the *Journal of Financial Therapy*,[5] "Financial Planners shoulder a great deal of financial and emotional responsibility when they manage client assets." As clients put their complete faith in financial planners to help them make wise investment decisions as well as to help them make personal, family, and business goals during market downturns, according to this report, "financial planners may experience significant levels of stress."

The S&P 500 chart from April to May 2009, as the Federal Reserve began an intense (and prolonged) period of injecting money into the banking system, similar to the Real Estate ETF chart, was in a strong Recuperation. The Federal Reserve is the central bank of the United States, incorporating twelve Federal Reserve district banks. The Fed raises and lowers short-term interest rates and the money supply to help control the U.S. economy.

That alone was enough to make me believe the "worst" was over. The spring of 2009 turned out to be one of the most opportune times that I can ever remember to make wise decisions concerning your money.

As the market recovered, interest rates dropped. Cash in the bank offered close to zero returns, and hoarding cash turned out to be the worst financial decision to make, while the returns in Real

Estate and the overall market since 2009 have more than doubled—if you knew where to look. Interest rates are the amount charged, expressed as a percentage of principal, by a lender to a borrower for the use of assets, commonly assessed annually as the annual percentage rate (APR).

My Career Change

After I left the Commodities Exchange in New York and returned to special education with the focus on inclusion, by 2009 I could see that the market had bottomed. I was a student of phases, and so I took the opportunity to join my husband's company, MarketGauge.com, and begin *Mish's Daily*, a newsletter, a Twitter account under @marketminute, plus a recommendation service for subscribers. The relevance here is that I made a career-change decision based on the very concept I am writing about in this book—phases.

The opportunities in special education in Santa Fe were limited. I was very lucky because I had been in the investment business when I worked on the New York Commodities Exchange as an independent trader, and my husband had a business I could grow into. Due to my knowledge of phases, I saw the market phase turning positive, which enabled me to head in the perfect direction.

Back to the Big 6

Going back to the cycles of how phases move, the Recuperation Phase happens to be one of my favorites since it taps into perhaps the greatest attribute of us humans—hope! After 2007–2008, during the intense Bear Phase, the switch into a Recuperation Phase tapped into that hope: hope that the economy would improve, hope that 2008 was truly "the darkest period before the dawn."

As you move clockwise on the circle chart in figure 3.1 from Recuperation, if situations continue to improve (and perceptions become more positive), the next phase is Accumulation. This is when hope becomes optimism. From there, call it a self-fulfilling prophecy, irrational exuberance, or anything else pundits say to dismiss any possibility of enduring "good times" (especially after PTSD), the phase goes back into a Bullish one. Naturally, all good times must deteriorate, which is when we see the phase go back into Caution, possibly Distribution, and then eventually back to Bearish. Oftentimes, economic cycles flip back and forth between a Bullish and Caution Phase or between a Bearish and Recuperation Phase for extended times.

Summary

1. There are six phases, all easily identified by the 50 and 200 simple Weekly Moving Averages.

2. Knowing the phase the market or any sector of the economy is in is like having GPS. Attaching an emotion or sentiment to each phase humanizes its impact on the market and overall economy.

3. Headlines are misleading and often too late.

4. You will no longer feel solely dependent on the media, your financial planner, or anyone, for that matter, to make smart and timely decisions about your money under any circumstances.

CHAPTER FOUR
MEET THE KEY
ECONOMIC COMPONENTS

A s a lifetime investor, I look for ways to become my own "armchair" economist. I want to decipher for myself and in real time how the U.S. economy is performing and then try to accurately predict how it will perform. I want to make these predictions not after the fact but well before the economic statistics come out. Whether the stock market runs ahead of the economy or can predict what the economy will do is debatable. Of course, the market can give investors false signals. Yet Douglas Pearce, professor of economics at North Carolina State University, who studied stock prices from 1956 to 1983, found that prices did generally start to decline two to four quarters before recessions began. In addition, he found "that prices will rise before the beginning of an economic expansion, about halfway through an economic contraction."[1]

Countless statistics are published each month. From employment numbers to consumer confidence to the gross domestic product (and way more), the number of stats is overwhelming and virtually impossible to track.

With a combination of one market index and five essential sectors and groups of the U.S. economy, you too will become your own "armchair" economist. In fact, for making personal money decisions, you will have a much simpler way than economists will have to figure out what is going on in the economy and how that affects your wallet. Together, these five sectors and one index provide an actionable and succinct way to assess where the money is flowing in the market. I like to think of them as my economic family, replete with both dysfunctional and fun times!

The economic family helps you gauge whether to be aggressive or passive on the buy and sell sides of the market. I like to focus on the harmonies and discrepancies of these sectors along with the Russell 2000. This helps with finding patterns and making connections. This family of sectors and groups shows you what is happening in the market with incredible precision because they perfectly illustrate just how the dance between the bears and the bulls endures.

The Market Index and Five Sectors: What Are Their Roles?

The Russell 2000 (IWM, its ETF symbol) is the best measure of the health of the U.S. economy. The ETF IWM is the financial instrument that represents the direction for this index. This index represents 2,000 small-cap stocks, which manufacture and distribute goods and services primarily within the United States. Small caps are companies with market capitalization generally between $300 million and $2 billion.

I like to think of the Russell as "Granddad"! With 2,000 stocks in this index, companies such as Etsy, Inc.; Weight Watchers International, Inc.; World Wrestling Entertainment, Inc.; Class A; Texas Roadhouse, Inc.; Crocs, Inc.; Sally Beauty Holdings, Inc.; Brookdale Senior Living, Inc.; and La-Z-Boy, Inc., represent the "meat" of the U.S. economy. Granddad helps you observe how the U.S. small-cap companies are performing. This information allows you to assess independently and effortlessly the pulse of the economy and the market. However, the IWM does not stand alone.

"Grandma" is the Retail sector (XRT); after all, she controls the family budget. As 70 percent of the gross domestic product (GDP),

Granny Retail tells us whether consumers are out there doing their part to stimulate the economy.

As an accurate measure of consumer confidence, the Retail sector must keep up with or lead the indices for sustained rallies. That makes Granddad and Grandma a perfect pair. If they are both performing well, most likely so is the overall market. If they are both feeling poorly, that is extremely helpful information. If they are going in opposite directions, take that as a sign of caution.

Granny Retail is in a "typical" mall within the United States. Stores such as Nordstrom, GameStop, Wal-Mart, Costco, TJ Maxx, and O'Reilly Automotive consider the shopping habits of most U.S. consumers.

To complete the economic family dynamics, Granddad and Grandma have four grown-up sectors (kids).

Brother Regional Banks (KRE) is the prodigal son. He has periods of wastefulness coupled with periods of high productivity; KRE tells us the borrowing and saving habits of the American consumer.

Regional Banks is a key sibling because he measures the health of the U.S. Regional Banks sector, where many local folks put their money.

KRE is sensitive to what the Federal Reserve might do regarding raising or lowering interest rates. It also helps market analysts calculate consumers' saving and borrowing habits. Regional Banks has a transgender sibling.

Transportation (IYT), with the prefix "trans," is a variable and ever-changing element of the U.S. economy. In today's world, the nature of how goods and services move through the economy is shifting with e-commerce and the internet. Nonetheless, how IYT is behaving continues to be very important.

If we go back in time, Charles H. Dow, cofounder of Dow Jones and Company, observed the patterns of what occurred in the markets during the Industrial Revolution, when the United States was a growing power. The Dow Theory is an analysis that explores the relationship between the Dow Jones Industrial Average (DJIA) and the Dow Jones Transportation Average (DJTA). When one of these averages moves up or down in price significantly, the other will follow.

The Dow Theory originated from his observations. The Transportation Index is a key component. Dow's first stock averages were an index of industrial (manufacturing) companies and rail companies. To Dow, a Bull market in industrials could not occur unless the railway average rallied as well, usually first.

We have come a long way since Dow's theory on how goods and services move. However, the notion of how much and how fast goods move throughout the country remains a critical measurement of the U.S. economy.

Biotechnology (IBB) is the manipulation or alteration of biological processes to create or modify commercial products and/or pharmaceuticals, and it made the cut for good reason; the anointed "Big Brother" IBB is a great way to assess if, how, and where money flows into the market.

Big Brother has many functions in the United States. He represents the pharmaceutical companies because of the power they have over us as consumers. Our current health and future well-being rely on Big Pharma. Big Brother wields power in Washington, D.C., as well. All the IBB holdings appear in NASDAQ.

IBB serves as a lead indicator of how much speculative money is flowing into the overall market. The more optimistic investors feel in general, the more they are willing to speculate in Biotechnology. The more they speculate, the better the outcome. If Big Brother is happy, that happiness becomes contagious. We typically see that spread to the rest of the other sectors.

Finally, there's the youngest sibling, Sister Semiconductors (SMH). The U.S. semiconductor industry has been a major innovator among all U.S. industries.

The semiconductor industry is the newest industry among my group. Economists estimate that all productivity growth during the current decade will be IT (information technology), based on both using and producing IT industries. Information technology is the application of computers to store, study, retrieve, transmit, and manipulate data, or information, often in the context of a business or other enterprise. The basis of the very growth of humanity is IT, and at its core are semiconductors. A semiconductor is a material or object that allows some electricity or heat to move through it, and electronic devices such as integrated circuits use them. They are the core of computer technology.

Per the analysis of data from the U.S. Bureau of Labor Statistics (BLS), the U.S. semiconductor industry now employs almost 250,000 workers directly and supports more than one million additional jobs throughout the broader U.S. economy. These supported jobs do not even include the millions of downstream electronics jobs in the United States that semiconductors enable.

Sister Semiconductors reminds us that automation, artificial intelligence, and big data are now a part of our everyday existence.

I refer to the "economic family" throughout this book. The important aspects for you to grasp to assess where the economy is and where it might be going are the phases of each of the sectors.

If the phases are all the same, watch for some level of diversion (which will be a lead indicator of the end of that synchronicity). If their phases vary or become disparate from one another, watch for some level of synchronicity to develop (and which direction they are all heading in). Whether lined up or disparate, how this one index and five sectors play out is the best overall indicator of the macro picture in the U.S. market.

Summary

1. The economic family is a combination of one market index (the Russell 2000) and five essential sectors and groups (Retail, Transportation, Regional Banks, Semiconductors, and Biotechnology) of the U.S. economy.

2. If the family members all trade in the same direction, it signals a great time to invest more aggressively. If the family is discordant, that is the best warning to invest more cautiously.

3. Each sector is "humanized" with a corresponding family title. These mnemonic devices give you an excellent way to gauge the macro picture of the U.S. economy.

CHAPTER FIVE
THE CONSUMER INSTINCT

S ome of my best financial decisions have come from going shopping and thinking to myself, "I better check out this stock, the store is insanely busy!" Or "I better check out this stock. I notice this chain is expanding its operations." Or even "This store has gone downhill. I wonder if this stock is ready to sell off." I have also talked to many people who never invested in the market before but made an investment decision after hearing about an innovator or a "hot" entrepreneur on the news.

Recently I dined at a local lunch spot in Santa Fe and spoke with a woman named Stevie. She had Elon Musk's biography (founder of PayPal, Tesla, and SpaceX) with her, which prompted our conversation. As it turned out, in 2012, after she heard about Musk and his selling PayPal and then taking that fortune to develop Tesla and Solar City (now owned by Tesla), she bought Tesla stock, at that time trading at $32.00. Tesla hit $384.80 in June 2017.

More frequently, though, I talk to people who really have no idea that their instincts are worth following up on, and even if they want to follow up, they have no idea what to look for.

What Is the "Consumer Instinct"?

Peter Lynch is one of the most famous investors in the world. A former manager of the Magellan Fund at Fidelity, he averaged a whopping 29.2 percent annual return in his day. Lynch's number-one philosophy on investing is *only buy what you understand*. He states, "If you stay half-alert, you can pick the spectacular performers right from your place of business or out of the neighborhood shopping mall, and long before Wall Street discovers them."[1]

According to Lynch, our research tools are our eyes, ears, and common sense. Lynch would get some of his best stock ideas in a grocery store or chatting with friends and family. He believed that we *all* have the ability to see emerging trends when we watch TV, read the newspaper, or listen to the radio. His reasoning is that since we consumers represent two-thirds of the gross domestic product of the United States, the stock market is actually in the business of serving us. If a product or service attracts us as a consumer, then it should also be of interest to us as an investor.

Lynch's research after his "common sense" kicked in was largely fundamental in that he studied sales numbers, earnings growth, and debt-to-equity ratios. As a primary technical trader using the phases, I tend to stick more closely to the information that the phase, slope, and price point indicate.

For the Women

My women friends are smart and amazing. They all work, have families, and function as the chief financial officers of their homes. It is no small feat; they all look amazing, too, and take great care of themselves!

Their jobs run the gamut from manager of the front desk of Sotheby's, head of human resources at the local hospital, medical doctor, author and writing coach, real estate investor and property manager, country and western singer/songwriter, chairman of the

board for Guiding Eyes, and director of trading education and research at MarketGauge (oh wait, that's me!).

Women and Investing

Although women have more patience and are more risk averse
than men, studies show that women lack confidence when it comes
to investing and financial literacy. Prudential's research titled "Financial Experience & Behaviors among Women" reveals that just 22
percent rated themselves as very well prepared for financial decision
making, compared to 37 percent of men. Yet women live longer;
therefore, they need to pay more attention to retirement saving and
financial planning.

Most of my women friends have IRAs or 401(k)s. Many of
them tell me they rarely look at the statements and have very little
understanding of the market. Furthermore, they go on to tell me
that money scares them. What's more, these are the smart ones!

Getting back to Peter Lynch and the consumer instinct, all my
women friends love to shop! I hope to pass on to you what has been
extremely successful for me.

Kohl's—A Personal Story

In December 2012, I went to visit my family in Bayside, New
York and East Rockaway, Long Island. My sister loves Kohl's, especially its cash-back program where you get a ten-dollar coupon for
every fifty dollars you spend.

We piled into her practical Honda Accord and headed over
to Kohl's to cash in on her coupons plus the additional 20 percent
Kohl's offers in its weekly circular. I couldn't believe the crowd!
There were throngs of shoppers—mainly women and children. The
cash registers and checkout clerks worked on both sides of the store.
The lines of shoppers waiting to pay extended all the way to the back
of the store and circled around.

Once I returned to Santa Fe, I visited a recently built Kohl's. It was not nearly as crowded as the one on Long Island; in fact, the store had merely a sprinkling of shoppers. I spoke to the store manager at the Santa Fe location and asked her how robust she thought sales were and whether she liked working for Kohl's.

I wasn't looking for an official quote of sales or a prediction of what the next quarter earnings would be; I merely wanted to hear the store manager's perception. She told me that she thought the store was doing very well given that Santa Fe's population is about 150,000. However, she told me she had transferred to Santa Fe from the Albuquerque store. Albuquerque's population is close to a million. That store, she told me, is doing extremely well. Incidentally, she loved working for Kohl's and felt they treated all of their employees well.

I asked her whether there was any sort of stock-buying program for employees or if she had any idea what price the stock was trading at. She stated that there was no stock-buying program and that she had no idea of Kohl's stock price.

The difference between the store manager and most of you (until now) and me is that I rushed home to look at a chart of Kohl's. In December 2012, the 50-WMA (dotted line) crossed beneath the 200-WMA (solid line) (figure 5.1). If looking to buy a company's stock, when the 50-WMA crosses beneath the 200-WMA, that signals weakness—hence, not the optimal time to consider buying the stock.

Considering the time of year and how busy the Long Island store was, the stock price was falling rapidly (notice the bars that drop from a price of around fifty dollars down to about forty-four dollars). Furthermore, the phase was definitely not Bullish. Is that the right time to either buy the stock or rely on Kohl's roseate future as the store manager and the crowds in New York led me to think?

Now, look at what happens to the 50-WMA by March 2013. The stock price rises above it and the slope of the 50-WMA begins to go positive, indicating a strong Recuperation Phase. Later on in

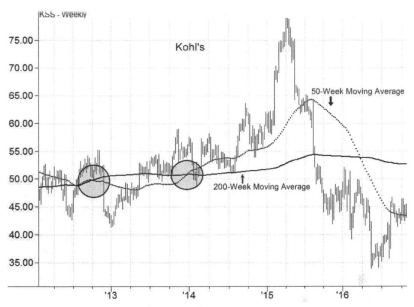

Figure 5.1. Kohl's September 2012–May 2016 (Courtesy of Trade-Station Technologies, Inc.)

March and into April, the price continues its ascent over the 200-WMA. The slope neutralizes at fifty dollars, where the price was in December 2012. For those who are looking to invest in a stock, the time for an initial buy was in April 2013. Equally legitimate, if you waited until the 50-WMA crossed back over the 200-WMA, you had a perfect scenario. Once the 50-WMA crosses above the 200-WMA, that is a signal of strength in the company's stock.

Although Kohl's stock ran up to around fifty-eight dollars in 2013, the more opportune time to buy that stock occurred in the beginning of 2014 when the 50-WMA crossed back above the 200-WMA. Imagine saying to your friends, "Guess what? I've been shopping at Kohl's for more than a year, and, finally, it is entering a Bullish Phase. Perhaps this is a good time to invest in the stock and/or send my high school–aged child there for a part-time job!"

Indeed, my consumer instinct required some patience. Yet it required no guesswork. Following the Bullish Phase, Kohl's stock rose to eighty dollars at its peak in 2015. Additionally, it held above the 200-WMA, keeping the phase intact.

Kohl's as of December 2015

What happened? I still love the store. So does my sister on Long Island. But talk about a fall from grace! Nearly two years from the start of the rally, the stock began to rapidly decline. The nasty declining bars show the drop from eighty dollars down to around sixty-two dollars in just a few weeks. Once it broke the 50-WMA, stockholders began to sell their holdings. That is why you see even more deterioration in price in the weeks ahead. In mid-April, the Kohl's stock broke below the 200-WMA.

Some folks might consider that a travesty for the store. With the ease of searching for information on Google (another super investment, using the consumer instinct), I looked to see whether there was any news of the company being in trouble. Seasonal sales in September were lower than expected. In spite of this, as of December 1, 2015, Kohl's announced that it was donating nearly $6 million for children in need.

What does that tell me? Look at the chart. If the price creeps back up over the 200-WMA again, the worst is most likely over. If not, you will know right away if the price cannot be sustained above fifty-four dollars. The best news is that with understanding phases, if you love Kohl's and its charitable organization, all you have to do is wait for the phase to be Bullish again.

Instinct Told Me to Sell the Whole Foods (Whole Paycheck) Stock

The Whole Foods in Santa Fe, New Mexico

Often, when I am out shopping, random thoughts come into my head about the store where I am spending my money. In December

2014, long before Amazon bought out the store, I was standing in the produce section in Whole Foods looking at the organic vegetables. They looked awful, certainly nowhere near the quality they should have been considering the exorbitant prices Whole Foods charges. (As an aside, if a product says "organic," "gluten-free," or "vegan," plan to pay even more.)

I was holding a soggy and brownish-colored baby bok choy with a look of extreme disappointment on my face while standing next to a couple who, at the same time, were holding some wilted spinach. I said aloud to them, "I think Whole Foods stock is a short."

Although a seller may not have owned stock in any particular company, the seller can short or sell stock in a company. If the seller believes the stock will go down in price and it does, the seller buys back the stock at a profit.

When I declare my thoughts about whether to buy or sell a stock of the store I am shopping at, I know one thing for sure: time to check the charts and the phases. Furthermore, I knew my own food-shopping habits were changing. When we first moved to Santa Fe, Whole Foods was my primary place to do grocery shopping. Over the years, however, not only were Trader Joe's, Kroger's (Smith's), and Sprouts getting more of my attention, but I could also see those stores getting more crowded with like-minded consumers, while Whole Foods's long lines for the cashier were beginning to shorten.

Typically, I like to ask employees their thoughts on the store: if it was doing well, how they liked working there, and so on. However, unlike Kohl's, Whole Foods had an employee stock-purchase plan, so I put my soggy bok choy back on the shelf and left without talking to anyone else.

In December 2014, I looked at the weekly chart for Whole Foods. It made a huge run up in October. As 2014 ended, the stock continued to price higher. It seemed that my instincts were off. But were my instincts inaccurate, or does it really matter when timing the follow-up on those instincts is just a matter of knowing how to follow phases?

In March 2015, the 50-WMA crossed below the 200-WMA to enter a death cross. In the ensuing weeks, there was (as we say in the trading business) a sea of red. In the week of May 8, the price fell below both the 50- and the 200-WMA. By the end of May 2015, the 50-WMA dropped beneath the 200-WMA, and Whole Foods entered a death cross and Bearish Phase. Both *death cross* and *Bearish Phase* refer to when the 50-WMA crosses below the 200-WMA, which indicates a move into a more Bearish Phase and is often a good sign that the price of the stock will go down.

If you were a trader or investor, once the price dropped below the key Moving Averages, you would have known to exit a long position and perhaps even sold short. If you were an employee of Whole Foods, depending upon how long you planned to stay, you now had the ability to determine the stock's phase and make educated decisions. If you were a consumer who enjoyed seeing that your instincts were typically correct, you gained more confidence to act on them in the future—bravo!

In February 2017, Whole Foods cut its full-year sales and profit forecasts after posting its sixth straight quarter of same-store sales declines. Management announced the closing of nine stores by April. That sounds bearish, right? Initially, yes. Then, in April, after the intended stores closed, the price roared, ending Whole Foods's Bearish Phase and sending it into a Recuperation Phase—another great example that the headlines come out behind the (technical) times.

In June 2017, Amazon bought Whole Foods for $13.7 billion at a stock share price of $42. That catapulted the stock price above the 200-WMA, or into an Accumulation Phase. So much for the soggy and brownish-colored baby bok choy—Amazon to the rescue! The Whole Foods stock is now under the Amazon umbrella; therefore the stock symbol WFM no longer exists.

Men Have This Instinct Too!

While I was busy capitalizing on my instinct to be negative on Whole Foods (while at the same time looking at their competitors, such as Sprouts, and tracking those stocks and phases), Keith, my husband and partner, was spying Amazon, ironically, long before the company bought Whole Foods.

At the same time, in December 2014, when thoughts turned to gift giving and holiday celebrations, we went to a party. The age group of the attendees was roughly forty to seventy-five, Baby Boomers and Gen X folks. Everyone there discussed shopping on-line at Amazon for virtually everything from toilet paper to jewelry to electronics. Since these are our friends, they all know that Keith and I are in the finance business, so naturally they all wanted to hear our thoughts on the Amazon stock.

Personally, and maybe because I work from home and spend all day on a computer, I like shopping on Amazon, particularly for price comparisons. However, I really enjoy going shopping at a mall or chain such as Kohl's, mainly to get out of the house, but also to have a full-on sensory shopping experience. Call it retail therapy.

Keith has spoken with me about the consumer switch from shopping at malls to shopping online, but this was the first time we heard our age group so resoundingly talk about doing so in such a matter-of-fact tone. When one is in the business and talks to friends, one learns that it is a no-win situation to give specific stock investment advice. If you give good advice, looking "smart" is meaningless since you are only as good as the last advice you gave.

We encouraged our friends to look at the chart in figure 5.2. In December 2014, Amazon was trading in a Caution Phase. That meant that although the price was under the 50-WMA, it was holding above the 200-WMA. The slopes of both Moving Averages were positive. That indicates that the Caution Phase is weak, perhaps from some profit taking (people getting out of their long positions) ahead of the end of the year.

At the end of October 2014, Amazon got close to the 200-WMA when the price got to $285. Then, in January 2015, Amazon's price fell once again to $285. At both points (although in January the slope was more positive), the 200-WMA came in

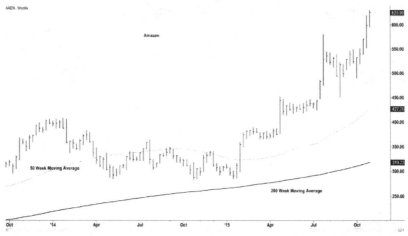

Figure 5.2. Amazon October 2013–December 2015 (Courtesy of TradeStation Technologies, Inc.)

around $275. For my more sophisticated investors, that is a very small amount to risk since the 200-WMA is often a reliable line in the sand. That means investors would most likely exit their positions if Amazon failed to hold the 200-WMA. With the slopes positive and the two bounces up from the $285 price level indicating buyers are coming in, it would certainly prove a legitimate signal that it was a good time to buy the stock for a position trade. A position trade is a trade that can last from months to years.

If you were thinking about a career at Amazon or wondering about what skill set you would need to work in a company like Amazon, the opportunity to become involved would be well worth it. By the end of January 2015, Amazon's price rose to clear the 50-WMA. Talk about a trade that can last for years. Amazon more than tripled in price, less than three years later trading up to and beyond $1,858 per share.

Use Your Consumer Instincts for Scary Megatrends Too

Since attention to viruses like Zika or to the swarm of Africanized bees that killed a poor hiker in Arizona in June 2016 has barely been on the market radar, I find myself a bit obsessed for two reasons. I have learned as a trader that when elements escalate beyond human control, they begin to occupy my mind. That is the time to think about the type of investments into which that might translate. I mentioned that I have two reasons for my obsession. Besides trying to make money, I worry. I worry about natural disasters such as tornadoes, floods, and drought. I worry about spreading illnesses. I worry about bees—in fact, I worry about them a lot because I am allergic to their stings. Yet, as I've been well trained to think about money opportunities at the same time, while I'm screaming for my EpiPen® I am also wondering which pharmaceutical company makes it. Thank goodness, no bees have stung me lately. I did, however, look up the pharmaceutical company that makes the EpiPen®.

Officially called the EpiPen® (epinephrine injection), Mylan, Inc. (MYL)—the third-largest generic and pharmaceutical company in the United States and the second-largest generic and specialty pharmaceutical company in the world—is the producer.

I hope that any thought about a product, a particular store, or a megatrend that comes into your head from now on leads you to do what I illustrate for you here—check out a weekly chart (two of the many websites that offer free charts are StockCharts.com and Yahoo Finance).

For example, let's say you were stung by a bee in late 2011 and saved yourself from an allergic reaction by injecting yourself with the EpiPen®. That prompted you to look at the weekly chart for its maker, Mylan (figure 5.3). You would have seen that the price sat below the 50-WMA but above the 200-WMA. By early 2012, MYL went into a Bullish Phase. The inflection point was palpable as the stock began 2012 trading below twenty dollars and within three years traded up to nearly eighty dollars! Not only was that a

Figure 5.3. Mylan Labs April 2011–January 2016 (Courtesy of Trade-Station Technologies, Inc.)

picture-perfect low-risk-buy opportunity for the stock, but it was also a good time to check out a career in what was clearly a growth company.

Now, let's say you got stung by a bee in October 2015. Bees tend to be sluggish by October, but it still hurt. So, you took out your EpiPen® to minimize any possible allergic reaction. After recovering from your sting, you checked out the weekly chart of Mylan.

Whoa. It is a completely different picture. There is a substantial drop in price that happened the week of July 31, 2015. That drop took the price beneath the 50-week Moving Average and into a Caution Phase. The continuing drop in price from that point shows how market psychology works. This shows that *when* you look at a chart dictates what action (if any) you should take.

The "herd" exited MYL over the next several weeks. Once the 200-WMA was touched, there was a bounce in price. However, the stock could not recapture the 50-WMA, which only brought in more selling pressure. Wavering between a Caution and Distribution Phase, you can see that the sharply declining slope on the 50-WMA threatens to cross beneath the 200-WMA. This is a death cross. The phase turns Bearish.

As you will read later, a Caution Phase is a great time to liquidate a stock. It could also be an excellent time to consider a change in careers or companies if you work for one that has a dramatic decline in stock price (such as Mylan had).

Summary

1. We all have a "consumer instinct" or a real sense about which products, stores, companies, and/or trends are "hot" or "cold."

2. Using phases, women and men alike now have a way to hone their instincts to make important investing and career decisions!

3. Take your personal shopping experiences and look at a chart to see phases. Then you are empowered to make investment or career decisions.

4. Megatrends are another way to help you make smart choices for your and your family's future.

CHAPTER SIX

THE BULLISH PHASE—EUPHORIA

Everyone loves a Bullish Phase! How do I know? For starters, it is the easiest chapter to write since there are investment and life-altering opportunities everywhere! In 1978, Merrill Lynch launched TV commercials showing a bull walking through a china shop. The bull became its logo because a bull implies something strong, commanding, and energetic.

The *Merriam-Webster's Dictionary* definition of *bullish* is "hopeful or confident that something or someone will be successful: optimistic about the future of something or someone."

A Bullish Phase is often the most prosperous time for everyone—investors and noninvestors alike. Furthermore, prosperity evokes positive feelings. Those feelings can resemble "euphoria," hence the emotional equivalent to the phase.

During a Bullish Phase, investors are generally making a lot of money. In fact, many analysts and stock traders will tell you that they make most of their money during this time because the Bullish Phase stimulates substantial buying in stocks and/or in the overall market. The term "bull market" refers to anything tradable, such as bonds, currencies, and commodities (like gold, oil, and soybeans).

The chart in figure 6.1 of the S&P 500 (SPY) during 2013 illustrates a classic Bullish Phase.

Figure 6.1. S&P 500 Bullish Phase 2012–2015

In the S&P 500 weekly chart from 2013, the dotted line is the 50-WMA, and the solid line is the 200-WMA.

During 2013, the uptrend was fully developed, and higher prices ensued. Although one rarely sees anything go straight up or straight down, as in the chart in figure 6.1, whenever the price of the S&P 500 fell, it was an opportunity for investors to buy.

For those who may not invest in the market, it was also a great time to make other types of life decisions such as buying a house or refinancing, career changes, and so on. Throughout 2013, SPY remained well above the 200-WMA.

In chapter 2, I talk about freight trains and momentum and how the 200-WMAs, which track a longer period of time, will hold longer-term momentum better and therefore are a more accurate indicator of a long-term trend. As the train engineer lugging a 200-car train knows, it takes a super-long time to slow the train down. In the case of the S&P 500 chart above, the train engineer never even slowed down. Note the 200-WMA. It chugged along going upward with a slope that inclined throughout the year.

How Do I Identify a Bullish Phase?

1. The 50-WMA (dotted line) is above the 200-WMA (solid line).

2. The slope on the 50-WMA should be positive with the 200 neutral to positive.

3. The price (what it costs in dollars to buy or sell something) should be above both the 50- and the 200-WMA. In figure 6.1, the price or cost of the S&P 500 was above both the 50- and the 200-WMA.

The 50- and 200-Weekly Moving Averages

On the weekly charts, "50-week" is slightly less than a year, while "200-week" is less than four years. For longer-term investment decisions such as deciding when to refinance a house or buy a car, or to gauge the phase in the intermediate term (one to four years), the Weekly Moving Averages are extremely reliable. The phases that develop on the weekly charts will keep you from second-guessing those choices for years to come.

The Headlines versus the Phases

Clearly, when looking back at the top headlines of 2013, there was not much to indicate that the market would make such a strong move higher. In fact, if you had listened to the news or financial analysts, you most likely did not know to take advantage of the incredible opportunities in the many economic aspects that 2013 offered. But if you knew how to read phases (as you are now beginning to), you could have ignored the pundits and probably would have had an amazing 2013, setting in motion financial decisions that you would still be reaping the benefits from today.

Top headlines of 2013:

1. Obama begins his second term as president of the United States. (Pundits had a field day with this event—some saw it as a good indication of continued economic growth, others as impending doom.)

2. After twelve months of drama, outgoing Fed chairman Ben Bernanke announced in December that the central bank would begin to taper its bond-buying program by $10 billion a month. (The overall market didn't even blink, but the Real Estate sector [IYR], sensitive to interest rates, did not fare as well, as shown by the weekly charts and 50- and 200-WMAs.)

IYR—Real Estate ETF Weekly Chart

To highlight the point that if you bought a house before 2012, you did not make a wrong decision, look at a more intermediate-term chart such as the weekly one in figure 6.2. Although Real Estate (IYR) broke the 50-WMA, a homeowner did not have any reason

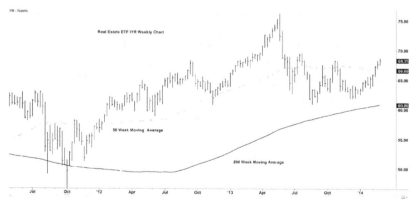

Figure 6.2.   Real Estate (IYR) Rally from Peak Low 2011 (Courtesy of TradeStation Technologies, Inc.)

to panic or experience buyer's remorse. If you look at August 2013, the weekly chart shows that the 200-WMA was well intact.

In October 2013, a partial shutdown of the federal government annoyed many Americans and dented an already weak economy. A bipartisan two-year compromise budget passed the House with overwhelming support on December 12. (Interestingly, there was a slight dip in the market in October, but it quickly recovered and continued rallying to the end of the year, although if you were listening to the news, you would have believed that the United States as we know it was dead.)

Perhaps you saw these headlines:

1. Gold ended the year at a loss for the first time in thirteen years.

2. The NASDAQ 100 ended the year at a thirteen-year high. NASDAQ 100 includes the world's foremost technology and biotech giants such as Google, Microsoft, Amazon, Intel, and Amgen.

3. Furthermore, during the same year, the Dow hit its fiftieth record high, with the S&P 500 right behind it.

4. The Duchess of Cambridge gave birth to Prince George Alexander Louis. (Great for the aristocracy of England— no impact on the United States, but it was nonetheless fun to read about.)

Gauging the Strength or Weakness of the Bullish Phase—or Slope

"When I see a slippery slope, my instinct is to build a terrace."

—John McCarthy

In chapter 2, I discussed how the 50 and 200 simple Weekly Moving Averages are what I use to determine which phase an instrument is in. The slope of these Moving Averages tells us a lot about how weak or strong a phase is. It is another easy layer of information to understand before you make any financial decisions.

The following may be a slippery slope for some. Technical terms can be daunting, and I promise you can easily see with your own eyes which way the slope is going—up or down. However, I find comfort in knowing that there are mathematical and thus provable formulas that make the concept of slope valid.

The Technical Definition of Slope That You Can Sink Your Teeth Into

Slope measures the steepness of a line. The slope equals rise over run. The rise is the up-or-down distance that a line travels. The run is the distance that the line travels from left to right.

In general, an advancing period has a positive slope and a declining period has a negative slope. The steepness depends on the sharpness of the advance or decline.

The slope can quantify the trend. A positive slope is by definition an uptrend. Similarly, a negative slope defines a downtrend. The slope does not predict the trend. Instead, it follows the trend or the price points. This means there will be some lag. However, waiting for a slope to turn from down to neutral or vice versa will help confirm how weak or strong that phase is and will show direction of the trend in case there is a change.

S&P 500: The Classic Bullish Phase 2013

Looking at the SPY chart in figure 6.2, we see that the slope on the 50-WMA was just beginning to have an upward slope at the beginning of 2013. As the year progressed, notice that the 50-WMA (dotted line) continued to incline in slope. Below the 50-WMA is the 200-WMA; notice that it kept a positive slope throughout the year as well.

Slope can gauge the strength of the weakness of the trend. A positive slope dictates a bullish bias, while a negative slope dictates a bearish bias. Directional movement can also be important when analyzing the slope. One way I like to determine whether a phase is starting to grow weary is by looking at any changes in the slope. If the phase is positive but the slope of the Moving Average is declining, that shows deterioration within an uptrend.

Best Time to Pay Attention to a Phase Change to Bullish Is the Golden Cross

A major goal of this book is to help you make many types of money decisions based on identifying phases. Never assume that if the overall market is in a Bullish Phase, all other aspects of the economy are as well. If you look back (as we did earlier in this chapter) at real estate, you saw that, contrary to the S&P 500, it began strong but soon collapsed under the 50-WMA. That is precisely why it's advantageous to look at each sector of the economy individually before making any assumptions or decisions.

Will you need to rely on the news? The experts? Perhaps your "smart" cousin who works for Goldman Sachs? Nope.

You Can Easily Follow Interest Rates by Looking at the 20+ Year Treasury Bonds (TLT)

The chart in figure 6.3 is the ETF for the 20+ Year Treasury Bonds (TLT). The TLT ETF is part of the NASDAQ. It measures the investment results that relate to the price and yield performance of the long-term sector of the U.S. Treasury market. It is by design very sensitive to long-term interest-rate movements. Treasury Bonds are a U.S. government debt security that pays a fixed rate of return with a maturity greater than ten years.

When Ben Bernanke was chairman of the Federal Reserve, he began the bond-buying program to stimulate the economy after the

Figure 6.3.   20+ Year Treasury Bonds 2009–2012 (Courtesy of Trade-Station Technologies, Inc.)

crash in 2008. That drove the interest rates down, making the cost of borrowing money much cheaper.

The Golden Cross

Where I have highlighted on the chart (figure 6.3), the 50-WMA crossed over the 200-WMA in a "golden cross." What makes the golden cross golden is the fact that it indicates a bull market is on the horizon.

A golden cross is when the 50-WMA crosses above the 200-WMA, and the price remains above the 200-WMA. This indicates a changed phase into a Bullish Phase and is often a good indicator that the price will go higher. Looking at this chart again for the Treasury Bonds, we see that it clearly broadcasted that the interest rates were dropping, and dropping fast!

Timing is everything, and now you have a way!

At the time the interest rates began to decline, putting the TLTs in a golden cross, the U.S. stock market, as measured by the S&P 500, took nearly another eight months to get going. The interest rate or TLT price had climbed from $95 (when the golden cross occurred) to $120 when the S&P 500 entered its Bullish Phase.

The Interest rates fell because of the actions of the central bank The banks began an aggressive policy to promote economic growth by buying government bonds, which lowers short-term interest rates and increases the money supply. The Federal Reserve, or the central bank, began purchasing Treasury Bonds in November 2008. By June 2011, the Fed had actively purchased longer-term bonds and mortgage-backed securities. The central bank continued the policy known as "quantitative easing" until October 2014. The interest rates have been near zero for years.

The extraordinary aspect of identifying phase changes on any chart or any financial instrument is that you do not have to be an economist or necessarily turn to the media for explanations of what is happening to any sector of the economy. All you need is a chart.

Summary

1. The Bullish Phase is when the simple 50-WMA crosses above the simple 200-WMA. The golden cross is the point of intersection.

2. The slope on both the 50- and the 200-WMA should be pointing up. The more the slope inclines, the stronger the Bullish Phase.

3. The price (or dollar amount) of the instrument should be above both the 50- and the 200-WMA.

4. The Bullish Phase empowers you make both timely and smart decisions about educational paths, career prospects, and investment opportunities. With just a little research, this information is literally at your fingertips!

CHAPTER SEVEN

THE BULLISH PHASE—NOT YOUR GRADADDAD'S KIND

The Great Bull Run of 2013

What Was the Decline in Interest Rates Telling You?

In the case of the TLT or interest-rate charts, having money in an interest-bearing account was *not* the wisest thing to do with your money, as you would not have received any interest at all for more than five years. Yet during the recovery period of the market and many sectors of the economy, the advice from many financial planners and advisors was to do just that: save your money. The "experts" touted putting your money in a bank and not making any investments.

According to Suze Orman, "All savings belong in a low-risk bank savings account or money market account. The goal is to keep your money safe so that when you go to use it, it will be there."[1]

Orman, to be clear, is not against making investments in the stock market. She says in the same blog, "Money you won't need to use for at least seven years is money for investing." She goes on to write, "Buy and hold (stocks) is the way to go." *Buy and hold* is when an investor buys stocks and then holds them over a long period regardless of what the overall market is doing. Tell that to the folks in

2008 who kept whatever money they had left in a zero-interest-rate savings account! I doubt that they would agree!

Buy and hold worked in the 1930s, but now, eighty-five years later, it is a whole new world!

Buy and hold ties up your investment money for years, making you believe that your money should only be available to you later rather than sooner. In today's world, easy access to, and the blinding speed of, information due to smartphones and other mobile devices has accelerated market trends from lasting years to only months.

Reading and understanding what to do (or not do) in any phase shows you that a buy-and-hold strategy is archaic, no longer necessary, and possibly costly. Following a Bullish Phase is an excellent way to avoid large losses and even make money, especially when your savings in the bank yields nothing.

Do You Have a 401(k)?

How many of you even look at your 401(k) or understand what it means? How many of you even know who is responsible for making decisions regarding your 401(k)? Many of you may think to yourself, "What does it matter? I have no control over it and all those financial planners are the same."

If you can read and understand which phase your investment is in, you can make informed decisions. In fact, I am confident enough to say that after reading this book, you might even have a better understanding than the so-called pros (unless they also read it!).

How to Find the Best Career Opportunities

If one looks at the charts of different sectors of the economy (such as Real Estate, Home Construction, Retail, etc.) and can see a phase change emerging, especially if it turns into a Bullish Phase, one can imagine that it means that that sector has potential for huge growth, thereby affording excellent job opportunities.

This information helps you discover not only what areas you should focus on for your investments but also which areas you should study for or get training in for a possible career change. It can also help a future small-business owner decide what type of business might be most successful and to get involved in it.

Where Should My Kids Go to College? What Should They Study to Ensure a Job?

Understanding phases will help you guide your children into areas of study they might want to focus on as they prepare for college and postgraduate curricula. Two great examples are Semiconductors (Technology) and Biotechnology.

Semiconductors—One Unbelievable Sector of the U.S. Economy

I spend a lot of time thinking about emerging trends, especially in areas where just good old common sense suggests that there has to be future growth because demand for the product or service will increase over time. In fact, some of our best investments began because we saw increased activity in a chain (like Kohl's) or went to a street fair and saw auto (Ford) representatives selling hybrids and electric cars. We get an idea from observing consumer habits, then check out the chart of the company.

In 2012, I began to think about Semiconductors because the use of electronic devices is here to stay and will most likely grow even more over time. I also hoped that with the manufacturing of semiconductors mainly in the United States, if the U.S. economy were to grow, these companies might prosper after a long decline.

Keith and I were in Denver after a two-week-long road trip through Wyoming and Montana, enjoying a cocktail at the bar of a nice boutique hotel. An odd-looking couple sat to our left. *Odd* because he was easily in his mid-sixties and she was more like twenty-something and definitely Russian (we could hear her accent).

We were close enough to hear their conversation, so, with a bit of eavesdropping, I made out the word "semiconductors"! I nearly fell off my chair. Unable to contain my enthusiasm, we began a conversation. Turns out, he ran a hedge fund and had made a long-term bet on the Semiconductors (SMH) chart.

That was August 2012. We got home in September and immediately bought the ETF SMH. If you look at figure 7.1, the 200-WMA became like a line in the sand. The price or dollar amount SMH traded in never crossed below that 200-WMA.

The moral of the story: In spite of the negative reports on Semiconductors and many other area of the economy in August 2012, we believed the charts and the Bullish Phase that was just beginning in Semiconductors. I kept a close eye on companies such as Intel to see how they would fare.

Timing Is Everything!

"There is a tide in the affairs of men which, taken at the flood, leads on to fortune."

—William Shakespeare

By 2013, many areas of the economy had begun to move higher, going into Bullish Phases. By January–February 2013, SMH began a

Figure 7.1. Semiconductors (SMH) October 2011–January 2015 (Courtesy of TradeStation Technologies, Inc.)

spectacular move higher. Notice in figure 7.1 how the slopes in both the 50- and the 200-WMA are rising. In March 2018, SMH's price peaked at $114.55.

Why Semiconductors?

Semiconductors are materials that provide conduction, typically between metals and ceramics. Most electronic devices, from your microwave oven to your television, use semiconductors. One of the most widely used substances in electronics is silicon. This is one of the major materials in semiconductors; hence the name Silicon Valley in California, where all of the influential tech companies have their headquarters.

The Weekly Chart for Semiconductors

In the Semiconductor chart, you see the same 50- and 200-WMAs. Each bar or line moving forward represents a full week. By the beginning of 2012, SMH touched down on the 200-WMA. The slope, though, on the 50-WMA was neutral until mid- to late 2013. Once the price rose above the 50-WMA, and the slope turned positive, the acceleration of the Bullish move increased dramatically.

For the purposes of illustrating the three criteria of a Bullish Phase, 2012 was perfect!

The three criteria:

1. Relation of the 50- to the 200-WMA

2. The slope on both MAs

3. Where the price sits on the chart

The 200-WMA is best for making intermediate- to long-term real-life decisions. To date, Semiconductors continue to remain a leading sector in the United States.

Semiconductor Companies in the United States

If you are looking for a job in the United States or have a child ready for college or technical school who has math and/or science aptitude, the following companies are located in the United States and therefore could offer opportunities for employment.

Intel Corporation, Qualcomm, and Micron Technology are the three largest U.S. firms (using largest revenue as criteria) in the semiconductor business. Samsung Electronics is the biggest firm located in South Korea. Other companies in the United States are Texas Instruments, Broadcom, and NVIDIA, to name a few.

What Type of Education/Training Does One Need to Work in Semiconductors?

Aspiring semiconductor engineers study chemical and electrical engineering. One can also go into research or university teaching. Computer science is another related field. There are websites that offer searches by subject, type of degree, or where you might want to go to school. One such site is Study.com.

There are also technical school certificates and associate degrees that provide education for semiconductor processors. However, employment opportunities recently decreased for processors because microchips have become too small for humans to handle. Therefore, it is wise to check into which area of semiconductors job growth is most likely to occur.

Currently, becoming an engineering technician is a good bet. More good news is that some community colleges offer certificates in just one year, and in some cases, certificates are applicable to associate degree programs.

With just a little bit of research, I discovered that one could have as little as one year of training or as much as a PhD for higher-level positions. I also discovered that according to Payscale.com, the median annual salary for semiconductor engineering technicians was $58,599 in 2014 but varied according to industry and location.

Incidentally, although I am focusing mainly on careers within the actual sector featured, if a company or group of the economy is prospering, these companies are most likely hiring for all sorts of jobs, including any type of support staff such as administrative assistants and even marketing and sales help.

What Does This Have to Do with Phases?

The bigger point is that just from tracking the Semiconductor ETF chart, I was able to see that the phase turned Bullish. From there, I was able to look a bit further and discover the top companies and what I might need in terms of training and education if I were interested in pursuing a career in the field.

Biotechnology—Largest Growth Area in the United States since 2012

What is biotechnology? The large concept of "biotech" or "biotechnology" encompasses a wide range of procedures for modifying living organisms for human purposes. It dates back thousands of years, from domestication of animals, cultivation of plants, and "improvements" to breeding programs that employ artificial selection, hybridization, and much more. Indeed, one may view the cultivation of plants as man's earliest biotechnological enterprise.

One of the classic examples of how our ancestors used biotechnology was the domestication of wolves. Breeding wolves for specific characteristics (that is, hunting and companionship) paved the way for man's best friend—the dog! Modern usage of biotechnology has multiplied exponentially, incorporating biological sciences such as genetics and cell biology, as well as further expanding into the world of pharmaceuticals.

The opportunities, from investment to education to career choices in this exciting area, have been and continue to be plentiful. Furthermore, although biotechnology is a field as old as man himself, it became extremely attractive in 2012.

The Bullish Phase at the end of 2011 perfectly depicts how one can make a plethora of good financial decisions from identifying phases and when they change.

The Biotechnology (IBB) ETF

The parabolic move in IBB really began in 2010 when the 50-WMA crossed over the 200-WMA, the golden cross. For those perusing charts in 2010 to hunt for opportunities for high school and college major choices, new careers, and career changes, the move in Biotechnology gave them a head start on one of the biggest upward moves ever!

In a way very similar to that shown in the Semiconductors (SMH) chart (figure 7.1), in January 2012, the move up really began as the slopes of both Moving Averages turned upward.

For investors, the risk level was still very good as the price remained near where the Moving Averages were. The best opportunity is when there is a classic phase change, and the price is as close as possible to the Moving Averages.

Education in Biotechnology

Imagine you have an adolescent at home. When the question "What do you want to be when you grow up?" arises, a blank stare is your only response. Here is what you and your teen can now do. Sit down and look at charts of ETFs that represent different sectors of the economy, areas of interest, specific publicly traded companies he or she might like, or even countries your child may dream of moving to one day.

Biotechnology has applications in four major industrial areas: health care (medical), crop production and agriculture, nonfood (industrial) uses of crops and other products (e.g., biodegradable plastics, oil, biofuels), and environmental uses. Biotechnology uses renewable raw materials and may contribute to lowering greenhouse gas emissions and moving away from a petrochemical-based economy. This is great news for those who want to work or invest in environmentally friendly sectors and companies!

Cool Stuff If You Need Financial Assistance

The National Institute of General Medical Sciences (NIGMS) instituted a funding mechanism for biotechnology training. Universities nationwide compete for these funds to establish biotechnology training programs (BTPs). Graduate students must compete for acceptance into a BTP; if accepted, the BTP provides a stipend, tuition, and health insurance to the student for two or three years during the course of their PhD dissertation work. There is also biotechnology training offered at the undergraduate level and in community colleges.

Biotechnology Careers and Related Career Options

A degree in biotechnology is not a one-way ticket into a lab coat. An education in biotechnology can set you up for a wide variety of careers, including management, marketing, and, of course, laboratory science. A career in biotechnology is entirely dependent on the highest level of education you have completed.

Biotech Companies in the United States

The top five biotech companies with headquarters in the United States are Gilead Sciences, Amgen Celgene Biogen, Idec Inc., Regeneron, and Alexion Pharmaceuticals. There are many more biotech companies, including those owned by, or a part of, pharmaceutical companies.

As with semiconductors, I did some research that directed me to specific areas of study, beginning in high school, that I might advise my kids to focus on. This time, I researched the types of jobs in biotechnology and which of those companies have headquarters in the United States for job applications. The research also led me to see which majors are applicable for both two-year and four-year colleges through postgraduate education. I was able to accomplish this in very little time because I could see the phase change!

When I ran the Pound Ridge Learning Center in New York in 1998, a big part of my job was college counseling and SAT tutoring. Therefore, I know how stressful this time can be for a family and hope that this logical guidance helps soothe some of the college and course-selection stress.

Earlier in the book, I spoke about the 200-car freight train and how much time it takes the conductor to brake before the train begins to slow down or comes to a stop. In the case of Biotechnology, the conductor has his foot on the gas pedal, meaning that the trend continues. As of July 2018, IBB held above both the 50- and the 200-WMA.

Healthcare (XLV) ETF

The chart for Healthcare in figure 7.2 shows a very strong trend up, with the golden cross in early 2012. This is a great low-risk investment in the ETF, using the formula of buying after golden crosses, with the slope in both Moving Averages pointing up and the price of the instrument trading close to those Moving Averages. Clearly,

Figure 7.2. Healthcare XLV December 2010–May 2013 (Courtesy of TradeStation Technologies, Inc.)

healthcare is yet another area that has a plethora of education and job opportunities. In February 2018, XLV traded a price as high as $91.78.

Summary

1. A Bullish Phase can be the best time to change the direction of your career or your child's life.

2. A look at interest-rate charts before deciding to keep money in a savings account or invest is as easy as identifying the phase.

3. An old buy-and-hold mindset is no longer necessary when you can track the phase of what you bought.

4. Semiconductors, Biotechnology, and Healthcare are just three examples of sectors where career and educational opportunities were available before economists predicted the U.S. economy's growth.

CHAPTER EIGHT
THE CAUTION PHASE—ANXIETY

There are many kinds of warnings. If we look at how humans receive warnings, according to psychology professor Michael S. Wogalter, PhD, at North Carolina State University, warnings come from a source. The source must transmit the warning effectively. The "warned" must be paying attention, comprehend the warning, and believe it. From there, the "warned" must be motivated to take action.[1]

In the market, when enough investors are sufficiently motivated, a switch in the collective behavior creates big moves. When the move creates a phase change, it is time to take note. The good news is that a Caution Phase (often the start of a collective state of fear) generally gives folks enough time to prepare, as they are exactly that—cautious—and not necessarily seeing a sign of impending doom.

Sometimes a phase will go to Caution only to turn back up to Bullish. In basketball or football, a player might lead with his head to pretend that he is moving in one direction only to stop and go in the other direction. Called a "head fake," the intention is to mislead the opposing team. In the markets, a Caution Phase that returns to a Bullish one is also a head fake and can potentially mislead the bulls.

However, do not dismiss false signals. In Formula One car racing, marshals wave different-colored flags during a race to communicate vital messages to drivers. A yellow flag indicates danger. The marshal gives one wave of the yellow flag as caution to drivers to slow down. Two waves of the flag means the driver must prepare to stop.

Whether a head fake or a heads-up, Caution Phases are usually an excellent time to watch and see whether times are changing.

In a Caution Phase, interest in buying in the market or any particular instrument begins to wane. The price plateaus. A Caution Phase suggests that upward momentum is slowing and investors are beginning to exhibit fear.

How Do I Identify a Caution Phase?

1. The 50-WMA (dotted line) is above the 200-WMA (solid line).

2. The slope on the 50-WMA is starting to flatten or turn slightly negative. The slope on the 200-WMA usually remains positive.

3. The price or cost in dollars is now below the 50-WMA but still above the 200-WMA.

The Russell 2000 (Granddad) or the iShares Russell 2000, with the New York Stock Exchange symbol IWM, is an exchange-traded fund (ETF). The ETF measures the performance of two thousand small-cap companies in the United States. The average market capitalization for the companies in the Russell 2000 is about $1.3 billion. Small-cap stocks over the longer term outperform medium- to larger-cap stocks by a wide margin.

The Russell 2000 Weekly Chart, 2013–2016

As already mentioned, the iShares Russell ETF is a well-diversified basket of small-cap stocks of companies that mainly manufacture within the United States.

Although it's not quoted nightly on the financial news, I consider the Russell 2000 the most reliable barometer of the health of the broader U.S. economy. Since it measures smaller companies that are almost all located and operating in the United States, in my daily blog, *Mish's Market Minute*, IWM received the moniker "Granddad" in my economic family. If IWM goes into Caution, I always take heed!

Figure 8.1 shows that the Russell 2000 was in a Bullish Phase until June 2014. For two weeks, the price broke below the 50-WMA. Notice that the slope on the 50-WMA was positive, making the Caution Phase a weak, albeit legitimate, warning that momentum could be slowing.

In October 2014 (denoted with Ellipse A), the price broke beneath the 50-WMA once again. The slope of the 50-WMA, however, continued to point upward. Although this time IWM went into Caution for several weeks, investors confidently came in to buy. At this point, with two slips into Caution within a few months of one another, I advised folks in my daily blog to watch Granddad carefully and modify Bullish sentiment to Caution. To me, this was a sign that the bull run in the market was ending.

Figure 8.1. The Russell 2000 March 2013–January 2016 (Courtesy of TradeStation Technologies, Inc.)

In the ensuing months, IWM ran up to make new multiyear highs in May 2015, making my cautious plea a bit premature. Yet seeing the run-up in prices only convinced me even more that the "irrational exuberance" was fishy after the two solid warnings. By August 2015 (denoted with Ellipse B), IWM broke the 50-WMA harder and faster. Judging by the slope of the 50-WMA, I knew that the third time was the charm. Where the chart ends (just at the beginning of 2016), the Russell 2000 continued to drop, approaching the 200-WMA, which was still sloping positively.

The Headlines versus the Phase

In June 2014, the top headline that sent the market into a minor decline had more to do with geopolitical uncertainty than the domestic economic news. However, the other two major headlines had to do with Federal Reserve policy and their take on the future of the U.S. economy.

1. Members of the Islamic State of Iraq and Syria (ISIS) take control of Mosul in northern Iraq, dealing the government an enormous—and unexpected—blow. ISIS continues to seize more territory, putting pressure on the United States and other nations to consider a military response. President Obama plans to send three hundred military advisors to Iraq but has no plans for deploying combat troops.

2. Federal Reserve chair Janet Yellen makes no guarantees about the future of interest rates and says that the state of the economy will dictate the future course of interest-rate policy. Although no change in the interest rates happened until December 2015, the stated intention to change policy was enough to spook investors.

   The Federal Reserve lowered the estimate for the gross domestic product (the total value of goods produced and services provided in a country during one year).

3. By the end of June, the market closed at a record high despite the Fed's warnings on growth expectations of raising rates. The Fed's lowered economic-growth expectations told the market that there would not be any surprise rate increases.

If your head spins just thinking about economic indicators, the reaction to them, and the subsequent regurgitation over and over by analysts attempting to interpret them, a phase cuts out all that noise. Charts help me navigate all the rhetoric of the Fed, economists, and talking heads.

The ETF TLT, established in 2002, comprises Treasury bonds with 20-plus years to maturity. By design, the TLT reflects long-term interest-rate movements. These Treasury bonds, issued by the U.S. Treasury, relate directly to rising and falling interest rates and therefore are a most reliable measure of where interest rates are heading.

It was plain to see that rates were to remain low while the future of the U.S. economy stayed uncertain. In addition, when geopolitical instability gets hold of the markets (the ISIS and overall Middle East situation continues to flare up), investors run into safety plays like Treasury bonds.

After seven years of an accommodative position (buying their own bonds), the Federal Reserve raised the interest rate for the first time in December 2015 by .25 percent. However, the TLT chart told us that as long as TLTs remained above the 200-WMA, the market (and the Federal Reserve) maintained a dovish stance regarding raising the interest rates.

Caution Phase, Bad News, and the Consumer Instinct All Line Up

Questions about the future health of the TV business emerged in 2015 as earnings in many media stocks tumbled. Disney peaked in price in August 2015. One year later, Disney's stock price fell by 29 percent. Here is a fine example of a sector of the market lining up perfectly with the Russell 2000's Caution Phase. Furthermore, consumers buying "smart" TVs, which reduced the desire for cable, gave me a heads-up on this before the earnings influenced the stock prices.

DISH Network (figure 8.2) flirted with the 50-WMA even before the official reports on Wall Street came out. In the last quarter of 2014 and in the middle of 2015, DISH broke under the 50-WMA but quickly recovered. I find that these early "warning" signs are reliable. Typically, it means the stock's upward momentum is starting to show fatigue.

By June 2015 (notice how similar this chart looks to the Russell 2000 chart), DISH failed the 50-WMA and hadn't recovered. Also, note that the slope of the 50-WMA began to flatten out and then decline. The Caution Phase accelerated.

Where the chart ends, the 200-WMA is close. Should the 200-WMA fail, further declines are expected. I love this example of how the perfect trifecta of headlines, consumer instinct, and the Caution Phase work together!

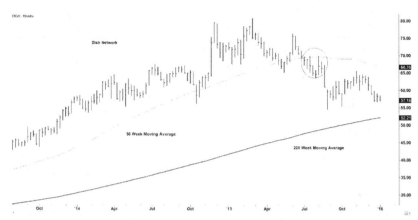

Figure 8.2. DISH Network August 2013–January 2016 (Courtesy of TradeStation Technologies, Inc.)

Summary

1. The Caution Phase is when the 50-WMA sits above the 200-WMA. The price, or dollar amount, works its way beneath the 50-WMA, yet remains above the 200-WMA.

2. The slope on the 50-WMA begins to flatten. As the Caution Phase gains momentum, the slope of the 50-WMA begins to decline.

3. Caution Phases follow a Bullish Phase in the natural progression of market and business cycles. Even if the collective behavior of investors turns to fear before the headlines do, somber headlines typically follow.

4. Caution Phases are an excellent time for investors and noninvestors alike to plan for a downturn in the market (and potentially in the U.S. economy as well). The Caution Phase is equally as empowering as the Bullish Phase. With a cool head, you can gauge whether you need to modify choices in an economic sector relevant to you, such as interest rates and real estate. You have the knowledge to make informed decisions about educational paths, career prospects, and investment opportunities well ahead of the curve. After learning about phases, you also have the confidence to look at your 401(k) and plan accordingly.

CHAPTER NINE

HOW TO AVOID THE THORNS

I've Been Duly Warned—Now What?

When everything is coming up roses, we look for the thorns to prick us. In a Bullish Phase, when the market is going up, it tends to rise on a "wall of worry." Symbolic of our psychology, where failure has been ingrained, we sit and wait for the good times to end. Whether it is self-fulfilling prophecy or the natural order of things, such is the case after a Bullish Phase. We know that a Bullish Phase will inevitably deteriorate into a Caution Phase.

Although the cock-eyed optimists are typically the last to throw in the towel, most of us are prone to fearmongering and begin to prepare for doomsday long before there is any real evidence of doom and gloom. That's precisely why I love the ease of identifying phases.

The Russell 2000: My Favorite Index

Previously, I used the Russell 2000 to illustrate how that index of two thousand small-cap U.S. companies is a reliable barometer of the "health" of the U.S. economy. As of August 2015, the Russell 2000 went into a Caution Phase. At the same time, so did the NASDAQ 100, S&P 500, and the Dow.

Shortly thereafter, all three of the three major stock market indices traded back above the 50-WMA and back into a Bullish Phase. The Russell 2000 did not.

I purposely covered the Russell 2000 because it went into a Caution Phase before the other three indices did. Even though it took months for the others to follow, I knew (or at least prepared for) the eventuality that the Russell warning was real, and the others would follow in kind.

Many investors doubted those warnings in the Russell 2000 because NASDAQ remained strong. Amazingly, after the August sell-off, NASDAQ rallied to make new all-time highs! The four main stocks in NASDAQ that led the charge were Facebook, Amazon, Netflix, and Google. Who can argue when the leading stocks are doing just that—leading?

In figure 9.1, I highlight the NASDAQ 100 chart (QQQ), the Dow Jones or top thirty Blue Chip Stocks (DIA), which are high-quality stocks of a solid company that typically is a widely recognized name—usually a market leader with $5 billion and up in market capitalization. The Russell 2000 (IWM) adds an interesting look at the comparison between how the S&P 500 (SPY) performed relative to the Russell 2000.

The ellipse in three charts shows how the price in the NASDAQ 100 and the Dow rose above the 50-WMA, while the Russell 2000 never rose back above it during the same period. The fourth chart shows that the S&P 500 ended 2015 on par with the Russell 2000. Once 2016 began, the Russell 2000 weakened significantly more than the S&P 500. Even where the chart ends, the Russell 2000 is down 11 percent, whereas the S&P 500 is down 6 percent.

The warning in the Russell 2000 not only gave me a heads-up on that particular index but also served as a reminder that phases are cyclical; therefore, the bull run could not last forever. With that in mind, a Caution Phase is a gift that allows you to get your ducks in a row, take inventory, and plug up any holes or reduce unnecessary

Figure 9.1. Comparison Russell 2000, S&P 500, NASDAQ 100, Dow Jones Industrial February 2015–February 2016 (Courtesy of TradeStation Technologies, Inc.)

risks should the caution lead to a real warning. And, I promise you, at some point, that warning will be real. It's the inarguable nature of cycles.

The market had already dropped 8 percent since the beginning of 2016. At the end of 2015, the S&P 500 closed out the year flat. Nothing lost, nothing gained. Had many financial planners understood phases and, in particular, how important the Russell indices are to the equation, imagine how well prepared they could have been in advance. Did your financial planner call you in August 2015 to tell you that it might be time to review your portfolio? What types of financial decisions can one make during the start of a Caution Phase?

What a Caution Phase Means for Your 401(k)

I often get phone calls from family and friends when the market starts a downturn. I am thankful that my friends and family are aware enough to know that they should start thinking about their

401(k)s. Part of the reason they pay attention is that they have a good friend and/or relative in the business and feel comfortable asking me what they should do. However, I worry about the folks who never open their 401(k) statements or, if they do, have no idea how to make changes.

During a Caution Phase, be sure you have a good understanding of your investments within your 401(k) funds. If your 401(k) is your retirement plan, it behooves you to take some time to investigate your options during a Caution Phase, especially since many investment plans have your money invested poorly for a downturn in the market.

If the 401(k) is the money you are counting on to put your child through college without debt, the Caution Phase is the perfect time to think about divesting some of that money. You might consider liquidating or reducing equity holdings. Or you could move more to cash, bonds, and defensive sectors.

Trust me—the "financial experts" do not always know what to do.

A financial writer for the *Washington Post*, like so many "gurus," publishes article after article about saving money. True, some 63 percent of Americans don't have money saved and have to borrow or incur debt should an emergency occur.

If nonsavers are the majority, then I wonder whether we need to reeducate the folks who can't or don't save in how phases can help them to invest, divest, or make informed life decisions. If you are in the 63 percent, I suggest you look at a phase or phase change in the market, a sector of the economy, or a particular company's stock.

In early February 2016, newspapers reported the anxiety retirement savers felt while the stock market declined. Investors were nervous not only about the market but also about flat wages, low interest rates, and marginally recovering housing prices.

These factors give many people an ostrich-like attitude toward even looking at their 401(k) statements. If they do look, older investors become so uncertain of their future that they figure any retirement before turning seventy is untenable. The well-intended Suze Ormans of the world keep telling us to save, but if only a minority are listening, isn't there a better way, one more in line with human behavior?

Another writer for *Bloomberg Business* published an article in January 2016, after the market had its serious decline, about how most people do nothing with their 401(k)s during market volatility. This got my attention. According to the article, nearly four million people contacted Fidelity about their retirement savings starting on January 4, 2016—a record.

T. Rowe Price reported a similar spike in phone calls or about 30 percent above the normal volume. Turns out, only 1 percent of 401(k) holders get out of equities completely during downturns. These folks call mainly to hear that they should "stay the course" and do nothing.

Of course, that is what they want to hear. Why? Because conventional wisdom says that if you sit through the downturn, eventual growth will reward you. I find all the advice confusing. Do nothing, save money, don't go into debt, and stop spending. The guarantee that everything turns around certainly applies to the eventual turn of phases, but is there any alternative to a passive approach? A perfect example is when in 2000 NASDAQ (QQQ, or the NASDAQ Composite Index) peaked at $4,289.06 in July 2000. Now affectionately called the "Tech Bubble," once QQQ went into a Caution Phase, a dramatic and costly fall in prices happened quickly. By October 2002, the composite index price fell to a low of $1,135.27. That is a 74 percent decline. What folks who might have bought at the highs lost in just two years took almost fourteen years to recover. By October 2014, the composite index returned to $4,289.

An even more spectacular example of how important it is to pay attention to phase changes and the Caution Phase is the Japanese stock market. On December 29, 1989, Japan's Nikkei Index peaked at $38,915.87. To date, or twenty-eight years later, the Nikkei has barely gained back half of those losses.

Do the Wall Street tycoons sit through major market swings and do nothing? I have learned to watch phases, anticipate when they might change, and then alter my investing style accordingly.

What Can I Do to Protect My Retirement Account during a Caution Phase?

First, know whom you should call once you see the major indices or any instrument in your portfolio holdings enter a Caution Phase. You will beat the throngs of panicked callers, for starters, and you might actually get someone on the phone to do more than reassure you, especially with your knowledge of phases! Also, note that, statistically, only 1.5 percent of T. Rowe Prices's two million 401(k)-plan investors made any changes when the market first tanked in August 2015.

What Can I Do to Reallocate My Holdings in My 401(k)?

First, if you plan to leave a company, you can transfer your 401(k) plan to an individual retirement account (IRA). That is a "rollover" and is not taxable or subject to penalties. If you have changed jobs often and have several 401(k) plans, consolidate them into one IRA account.

Second, educate yourself about the types of investments you can make. For example, a target-date fund is a mutual fund that allows you to pick a date that you think you will retire on. However, if you want some control over your investments, my advice is to stay clear of that type of mutual fund, as they are mainly best for hands-off investors.

ETFs

One question to ask is whether your plan is invested in exchange-traded funds. ETFs have lower operating costs and provide flexibility, such as in buying ETFs that profit on the market going down. There are bond, stock, international, and sector ETFs. I highly suggest you find a free charting service such as StockCharts .com if you do not already have a trading platform so you can see for yourself what phase any ETF is in.

How to Use Stock Charts (If You Do Not Have a Trading Platform)

1. Type www.stockcharts.com into your internet browser.

2. In the top left, type in the symbol of the stock or ETF you want to see.

3. Right next to that, click on the arrow and select "weekly" for "Period."

4. After you make any change to the chart, click on "update."

5. Below the chart is "Chart Attributes." Make sure the "Period" says "weekly." You can select "up color" as black and "down color" as black.

6. Click next to "Volume" to say "off." Then click on "Update."

7. Overlays—you want to see Simple Moving Averages and two parameters: 50 and 200. Click "Update."

8. Indicators—Click on "Clear All" and then "Update."

Notice that the Apple (AAPL) chart in figure 9.2 shows that AAPL is in a clear Bullish Phase.

401(k)s That Offer an SBDA Option

Your 401(k) plan may offer a brokerage window or a self-directed brokerage account (SDBA) option. Many employees do not understand how to evaluate mutual funds, so they go with default

Figure 9.2. Sample StockCharts.com Apple Inc. (Courtesy of Stock Charts.com)

funds. If you chose a preselected fund, you may not know about the self-directed option. This option allows you to designate an amount of your funds (could be up to 50 percent) to be placed in the hands of an approved financial advisor. That means you can find one with a good record. Even better, you can ask an advisor to read this book. After both you and the advisor understand phases, it should be a lot easier to make sound investment decisions.

The takeaway is that the Caution Phase does not have to be a time of complacency. Even if you decide to do nothing and sit through a negative cycle, I encourage you to at least be aware of what that means for your money.

Using the Caution Phase to Make Smart Career Choices

Did you receive notice that the company you work for might be giving out "pink slips" or closing stores? In the months after the Russell went into caution, Wal-Mart, for example, announced it was closing nearly three hundred stores worldwide. Interestingly, Wal-Mart went into a Caution Phase long before the Russell did. If you had a job there (they are the largest employer in the United States) in the spring of 2015, or thought about getting a job there, the chart gave you information about the future of the company.

Just as I showed you that the Russell 2000 had had a couple of false breakdowns below the 50-WMA, only to return above it and then rally further, so too did Wal-Mart (WMT; see figure 9.3).

Ellipse A exemplifies two important concepts about phase changes. The first concept is that a phase can continue to waver between phases (Bullish to Caution and back to Bullish in this case) for months or even up to a year. Furthermore, as I illustrated with the NASDAQ chart (figure 9.1), the price can run to the upside thereafter. Here, Wal-Mart exploded higher in the beginning of 2015 as sort of its last blast until the thunderous fall back to earth in mid-2015.

Second, in order to gauge the strength or weakness of the phase change, check the slope of the 50-WMA; throughout the erratic price movement shown in Ellipse A, the slope of the 50-WMA remained positive.

Now, if you look at Ellipse B, you see a different picture. Not only did the slope on the 50-WMA neutralize, but it eventually turned negative. Ellipse C shows how the stock went from Caution to Distribution. From there, it was downhill all the way. Ellipse D is a death cross or the start of a Bearish Phase.

Employees and Their Company's Stock

Typically, Wal-Mart employees do not follow the stock price, as they do not have a stock-sharing plan. Employees may not consider the possibility of making any investment in the company's stock. However, there is no reason why Wal-Mart employees should not consider buying or shorting the stock of the company they work at. It's not a matter of how much or how little salary an employee makes. It is a matter of getting in with the lowest amount of risk and watching the phases and the slopes of the Moving Averages.

Minimum Wage and Stock Price

On January 20, 2016, Wal-Mart Stores, Inc., announced that they planned to raise wages of more than 1.1 million employees to retain employees and improve the quality of its stores. Hourly employees would get a raise to at least ten dollars an hour, and the new minimum wage for top-level hourly employees would increase to fifteen dollars per hour. Of course, the caveat was that the company could reduce the number of hours an employee worked to compensate. Nonetheless, as you can see in figure 9.3, Wal-Mart was in a Bearish Phase. Make no mistake, the bottom line for Wal-Mart was attracting investors to buy their stock. They would do whatever was necessary to make sure profits rose.

The weekly chart, and particularly the 50-WMA, was all you had to watch to see whether the phase could improve from what figure 9.3 highlights as Bearish into a Recovery.

How Do I Use This Information for Other Companies?

Regardless of which company you work for, if it is a publicly traded company on the stock exchange, you can look at a weekly chart to see what phase it is in. You can assess the strength or weakness of that phase by looking at the slope of the 50- and 200-WMAs.

You will then have the technical knowledge you need to ask the right questions. If feasible, you can go to upper management at your company and ask whether there have been layoffs in any of the other stores or branches. You can ask whether any of the domestic

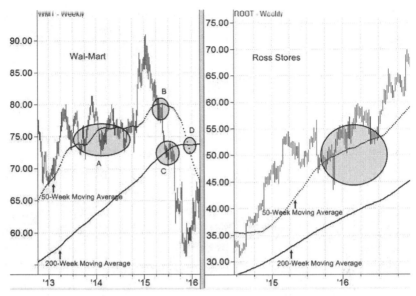

Figure 9.3. Wal-Mart August 2012–January 2016/Ross Stores February 2014–August 2016 (Courtesy of TradeStation Technologies, Inc.)

or global stores have closed or are planning to close. You can also use the phases to find other similar chains that might be in better shape. Remember the consumer instinct? Perhaps you shop at Ross Stores. Remember, when you search for a new job, sell your skill set to a new potential employer.

If concerned about your job at Wal-Mart, but you like Ross Stores, the chart shows a different picture. At the same time that Wal-Mart's stock was entering a Caution Phase (which quickly continued to deteriorate even more negative phases), Ross Stores (ROST) continued the climb that began in 2013.

The ellipse in figure 9.3 shows that the price of the stock dropped down below the 50-WMA. Considering that the 50-WMA maintained an extremely positive slope, it is no surprise that the price bounced right back up again. While Wal-Mart continued to fall, Ross Stores continued to rise.

With just a little bit of research and with the ease of Google, you can find out which companies are hot and which are not. For example, I searched "recent headlines" for Ross Stores on Google and found the following on March 1, 2016:

"Secrets of Women Shoppers: The Retail Stocks They Love"

In January 2016, Ross Stores, Inc. (NASDAQ: ROST), reported that the earnings per share for the fourth quarter were up 10 percent from the prior year. Sales for the fiscal 2015 fourth quarter grew 7 percent to $3.251 billion.

In February 2016, *Forbes* reported that Ross, like other discounted-apparel companies, had difficulty selling items online. However, as Ross expanded into digital marketplaces, the company created opportunities to sell to international customers.

Ross earned the label "Rocket Stock" for 2016. With e-commerce a growing trend among women consumers, companies like Under Armour, Lululemon, Athleta (under the Gap brand), and L Brands are growing as well. Ulta, the beauty retailer, is the leader of the pack, with both in-store and online shops growing appreciably.

All of these companies have weekly charts. You can look at any of these companies and make educated decisions about where to look for a career in retail or possibly to switch from your current job into a faster-growing company before you get that "pink slip."

Guiding Your Children's College and Career Choices

The generation born between 1982 and 2004 is referred to as "Millennials," "Generation Y," and the "Next Generation."

The largest generation in the United States, representing one-third of the total U.S. population, stands out as the most diverse and educated generation to date. Perhaps the most important marker for Millennials is that many of them have come of age during a very difficult time in our economy, as the oldest Millennials were just twenty-seven years old when the recession began in December 2007. As unemployment surged from 2007 to 2009, many Millennials struggled to find a hold in the labor market. They made important decisions about their educational and career paths, including whether and where to attend college, during a time of great economic uncertainty. Their early-adult lives have been shaped by the experience of establishing their careers at a time when economic opportunities were relatively scarce.[1]

No doubt, guiding your young Millennial into a career or educational path during a Caution Phase, such as the one that began at the end of 2015 and accelerated in the beginning of 2016, presents some challenges.

Overall, research finds that macroeconomic conditions in childhood and young adulthood shape individuals' trajectories for years to come and can have lasting impacts on wages, earnings, savings, and investment patterns, along with trust in institutions.[2]

Half of the Millennial generation expresses interest in becoming entrepreneurs. Contributing to society also rates high among Millennials. Another interesting fact stated in the above-cited report is that more Millennials earn college and postsecondary degrees than any other generation before them.

How the Phases Help You Guide Your Kids Away from Declining Fields into Ones That Are Stable or Growing

Social sciences is a growing field among Millennials. With the growing interest in making a difference, I researched the top public affairs schools for social policy to see what areas of major study are required in order to obtain a degree. The five most popular majors for 2014 graduates were biology/biological sciences, general economics, political science and government, general psychology, and speech communication and rhetoric. That sure confirms the research cited above about Millennials' desire to become more socially and community minded!

I researched the best jobs for social science majors by salary potential. The top job title is vice president of government affairs, requiring a political science degree. The other job titles range from analytics major to financial planner to criminal investigator to corporate paralegal. Fundraising manager, billing analyst, and registered sales assistant also made the list.

This field of interest among Millennials generated an impressive list of jobs along with a multitude of skill sets and postsecondary education requirements. Doing this sort of research with your child and/or with a college counselor makes sense as the first part of college decision making.

Perhaps more than ever before, current research shows that the single most important determinant of a person's income is their level of education. And, as the most educated generation in history, this will tend to boost earnings for Millennials over the course of their lifetimes.

Using Phases to Rank Publicly Traded Companies in Social Sciences

I investigated publicly traded companies and ETFs related to psychology, economics, sociology, social policy, and education to see which ones are in Caution Phases. Note: One good source to look at for a list of companies by industry is http://www.ranker.com/fact -lists/companies/industry.[3] Some are publicly traded companies and others are not. However, if you are looking for a list of educational companies to determine the ones that are the largest and most profitable in the world, this is a good resource. If you or your children are interested in working in the education field, you might want to look at these companies to apply for jobs.

Another great resource for information on publicly traded companies is investorguide.com. They provide a list of major stock market industries and allow you to browse by sector, industry, or letter.

How I Found Two Companies, One in a Bullish Phase, One in a Caution Phase

First, I searched the industry sectors on investorguide.com. I looked at the management services industry and found many disciplines that include careers in the social sciences. Of the five companies listed, I looked at the first one listed: Exponent, Inc. The stock symbol is EXPO. The company "evaluates complex human health and environmental issues to find cost-effective solutions." It is located in the United States and has careers in engineering, environmental, and health sciences, plus several other sciences and sectors from which to choose.

Second, I clicked on Careers. It told me how to apply and which career opportunities it had available. Okay, I am intrigued. However, before I send my daughter's résumé or encourage her to major in environmental forensics, I want to know how Exponent, Inc., is doing or what phase the stock is in (figure 9.4).

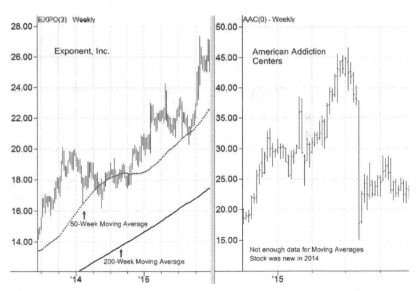

Figure 9.4. Exponent, Inc. May 2013–April 2016/American Addiction Centers October 2014–March 2016 (Courtesy of TradeStation Technologies, Inc.)

Considering that we just learned that the Russell 2000 and many other companies are in Caution Phases, it is good to see that Exponent, Inc., is still in a Bullish Phase. Furthermore, the slope on the 50- and 200-WMAs remains positive. This is encouraging for the industry, this company, and your child's future.

I then selected Specialized Health Care as an Industry Group. The first name on that list is AAC Holdings, or American Addiction Centers. The stock symbol is AAC. They provide inpatient abuse-treatment services for individuals with drug and alcohol addiction as well as food addictions. They are located in the United States.

The website took me to Careers. From there I clicked on "Regular Full-Time Job Opportunities." With six pages of job titles, I found that one could apply for anything from administrative assistant to behavioral health technician to senior corporate paralegal to outside sales treatment consultant.

From there, you can find out what specific education, experience skills, and abilities are required for each job. There is a plethora of opportunities for any Millennial interested in pursuing this field of social sciences.

How Is the Company Doing?

The best way to find out how the company is doing is to check the stock chart of the weekly price movement to determine the phase.

In August 2015, AAC went public. Since we need 50 and 200 weeks of trading data before we can see the 50- and 200-WMAs, this stock has not traded long enough for us to see the phase. However, it is easy to ascertain that 2015 was not a good year for the shareholders of this company.

If you look for a phase in a company and there is not enough information, you can at least tell whether the company looks to be rebounding. In this case, in early 2016, the price reached a new low since its public offering and is beginning to rise from there. I would not say that you should avoid working there, but I might keep an eye on the price over time to see how the company progresses. Overall, the opportunity at Exponent, Inc., appears to be the better of the two as the chart indicates a more sustainable growth environment.

What about Interest Rates, Home and Student Loans, and Real Estate Decisions?

The report "Millenials: Who Are They, How Are They Different, and Why Should We Care?"[4] states as fact that Millennials are less likely to be homeowners than previous generations. The reasons for this include higher college debt (which surpassed $1 trillion at the end of the second quarter in 2014) and higher unemployment (8.6 percent as of September 2014). By the end of 2015, 40 percent of the U.S. unemployed were Millennials. This translates to about 4.6 million young people out of work and a rising median age to get married (in 2013, only 30 percent of twenty- to thirty-four-year-olds were married, compared to 77 percent in 1960).

These are all valid statistics that explain why Millennials live with their parents (31 percent in 2014) longer, making them less likely to buy their own homes. Moreover, the current tight lending environment, particularly since Millennials tend to have more instances of lower FICO scores (67 percent of those under thirty have scores under 680), affects the ability to obtain a mortgage.

Millennials are also more likely to move into urban areas. Over the last thirty years, the college-educated group of twenty-five- to thirty-four-year-olds has been increasingly living in cities. The non-college-educated have also increased in city-living populations, although not as rapidly as those with a college education.

Caution Phase 2016—A Unique Dichotomy between Rates and Home Prices

Whether you are a Millennial who wants to buy a home, a Millennial who just wants information, a member of Gen X, or a Baby

Boomer, the opportunity to own or refinance a home was unique in 2016. In the spring of 2016, the price of the Real Estate ETF (IYR) was under the 50-WMA. That put it in a Caution Phase. Although it had traded under the 200-WMA, the price action showed it was trying to hold on for dear life.

One takeaway is that although housing prices were trying to stabilize, when IYR is in a Caution Phase, there is a possibility of housing prices going lower.

How Does This Relate to the Interest Rates or 20+ Year Treasury Bonds?

Meanwhile, the 20+ Year Treasury Bonds (TLTs) were in a Bullish Phase. That meant that interest rates for borrowing money were improving.

Typically, rates had remained low during the Caution through Bear Phases in the overall market indices. If you were holding cash or were part of the generation of savers rather than investors, that gave you a double-edged sword with which to contend. A good time to borrow money is when interest rates are low, especially if cash is not paying any interest in bank accounts. Looking for low-cost opportunities to buy and refinance makes sense.

If you have enough equity in your house, you can refinance. You can use that money to buy more real estate, especially if you can buy a house cheaply and sit with it should the value decline further. This is especially true if the area where you buy a house has a decent labor force; renting the house out should at least keep your cash flow neutral, and it may even give you a positive cash flow.

If real estate prices are depreciating, then doing a straight refinance is fine. It just means that you pay a lower interest rate than you are currently paying. Make sure, though, that after closing expenses, the savings pay off after a decent amount of time. In other words, if, after refinancing, your mortgage payments go down by $200 and closing fees cost $2,000, it will take you ten months to break even. After that, you start saving that $200 a month.

I look at housing opportunities as investments, provided you buy low and can sit for the long term. Rental markets might improve if people lose jobs and homes but still need a place to live. Do be careful investing in depressed cities, though; they could be the last to come back (if indeed they ever do).

What If My FICO Scores Are Bad?

There are multitudes of services that will help with advice on improving your credit scores. If you are burdened with student loan debts and cannot make your monthly payments on time, this will lower FICO scores, so consider asking the lender for a deferment.

Opting to defer student loans is not as ideal as repaying them, because it simply delays the inevitable, but it won't hurt your credit score. In fact, financial institutions may consider your deferment when deciding whether to approve your loan request. Lenders may come to the conclusion that you have enough money to pay back the loan they are offering you, since part of your income wouldn't have to go toward repaying student loans immediately.[5]

Watch the Headlines for Mortgage News

On February 22, 2016, Bank of America announced it would offer mortgages for 3 percent down as opposed to the usual 20 percent down ordinarily required. Their new loan program aims to help low- and moderate-income borrowers get loans up to $417,000. The required credit score is 660 or higher. One caveat, though, is that the less money you put down on a house, the larger the mortgage you will have to finance. You could be put at risk should the housing market continue to decline, as shown in the real estate chart in figure 6.2. It means you will have even less equity in your home.

Summary

1. A Caution Phase is a gift that allows you to get your ducks in a row, take inventory, and plug up any holes

or reduce unnecessary risk should the warning be a real warning.

2. Regardless of which company you work for, if it is a publicly traded company on the stock exchange, you can look at a weekly chart to see which phase it is in. If it is in a Caution Phase, you will then have the technical knowledge you need to ask the right questions.

3. All generations, particularly the Millennial generation, can use the phases to help make educational decisions regarding which fields to study. Looking at a company traded on the stock exchange will give you extremely valuable information about how the company is doing and what you might expect as far as the company's potential.

4. You can now make informed decisions without relying on the so-called experts regarding buying or refinancing a house and how that relates to the phase of the housing market and the current interest rates.

CHAPTER TEN
THE DISTRIBUTION PHASE—FEAR

*M*erriam-Webster's Dictionary defines distribution as "the act of giving or delivering something to people, stores, or business." The other definition is "the way that something is divided or spread out." In a Distribution Phase and after the glaring signs of the Caution Phase, one can surmise that as things deteriorate further, we literally see a distribution or redistribution of wealth.

The Distribution Phase gives something to people, stores, and businesses all right. It gives them an increased sense of doom. That is, of course, if you are unprepared.

In a Distribution Phase, it becomes clearer that business conditions, according to the market indices or a particular instrument, are getting worse. The overall sentiment turns more negative, and selling increases while buying dries up.

As you will see, many institutional players in the market begin to dump their long positions as they gauge the end of an uptrend during the Distribution Phase. Institutional investors are large organizations, such as mutual fund managers, hedge fund managers, banks, pension fund managers, labor unions, or insurance companies, that make substantial investments on the stock exchange.

Some hedge funds can take short positions, betting the market will continue lower.

As a very emotional time for the markets, investors can experience periods of complete fear interspersed with hope. If the Distribution Phase accelerates due to negative geopolitical events or extremely bad economic news, everyone gets nervous. Oftentimes the media have a field day during a Distribution Phase. Bad news sells, and fear increases media ratings.

However, since we were already "duly warned" during the Caution Phase, the Distribution Phase is not a shock. In fact, I find some solace in knowing the phases are following their natural cycle. We now have information and can prepare. We can even make money.

How Do I Identify a Distribution Phase?

1. The 50-WMA remains above the 200-WMA.

2. The slope on the 50-WMA usually goes from neutral to declining. The 200-WMA might also be declining in slope.

3. The price is below both the 50- and the 200-WMA.

In the last chapter, I illustrated the Russell 2000 (IWM), or the index that represents a basket of two thousand small-capitalization companies. The number of outstanding shares multiplied by its share price determines capitalization. That number represents the stock market's estimated "value" of the company. Small-cap companies typically have a capitalization of $300 million to $2 billion. That means these two thousand companies are relatively small compared to a company like Apple (AAPL), which has a market capitalization of about $557 billion.

As mentioned earlier, I have come to rely on the Russell as my best barometer and predictor of how the other indices will eventually perform. I am not alone. Many investors watch the Russell, as it is often the first to reveal details of the market psychology. Reputedly, small caps tend to underperform when bull markets top out and turn lower. That is exactly what happened in August 2015.

The Russell 2000 in a Distribution Phase

Figure 10.1 shows that the Russell 2000 entered a Distribution Phase, highlighted by the ellipse. Notice that the overhead dotted line or the 50-WMA has a sharply declining slope. The solid line or 200-WMA, however, has a positive slope. The conclusion drawn is that although the Russell is weakening, the Distribution Phase has not developed any real legs.

Furthermore, after an initial drop in price right after IWM broke down under the 200-WMA, it proceeds to run right back up. It could very well stop at the 200-WMA and turn back down. It could also continue to rise in price and head back over the 200-WMA and back into a Caution Phase. That back and forth between phases is common when the markets are declining. Value investors, or those who like to buy securities that are undervalued, come in looking for bargains. Sellers who sold during the Caution Phase or at the beginning of the Distribution Phase begin to buy back their shares.

The Headlines versus the Phases

The end of 2015 and beginning of 2016 saw many frightening headlines. Talk of recession dominated, which led to a record-setting number of phone calls to advisors by panicked investors. My intention in the Caution Phase chapter (chapter 8) is to prepare you for the inevitable "scare" well in advance. By the time you see horrible headlines, you will have taken precautionary steps.

Preparing for the worst well ahead of the curve proved worthwhile when, toward the end of 2007, my dear Granddad Russell 2000 jumped around in price, trading above and below the 50-

Figure 10.1. The Russell 2000 Distribution Phase 2016 (Courtesy of TradeStation Technologies, Inc.)

WMA. By the end of 2007 and beginning of 2008, the slope on the 50-WMA began to decline. Even after a few attempts at breaking and then recapturing the 200-WMA, the slope on the 50-WMA relayed that trouble was looming.

Even if you weren't as smart as the guys featured in the movie *The Big Short*, who capitalized on the housing-market bust, with a simple look at the charts and the phases, along with noting the declining slope on the 50-WMA, you at least could ascertain that trouble might be brewing.

When the huge decline happened in September–October 2008 and the news of the Bear Stearns and Lehman Brothers banks hit the tape, we were in all cash.

Wouldn't it be amazing to have had a crystal ball to look into? In 2008, the Real Estate ETF (IYR) not only went into a Distribution Phase but also fast-tracked into a Bearish one. Both the 50- and the 200-WMA had negative slopes, and the rest, as they say, is history. Then, at the beginning of 2016, IYR reentered a Distribution Phase ever so briefly. What does our crystal ball tell us?

Although the price action returned over the 200-WMA, the slope on the overhead 50-WMA remained negative while the slope on the 200-WMA remained steady and strong.

During the same period, headlines for Real Estate read.

"New Home Sales Fall Sharply in January 2016"
"Mortgage Applications Down 4.3 Percent"
"Spring Housing Season Kicks Off with Short Supply"
"Mortgage Rates Could Cross a Record Low"
"Rising Mortgage Rates Could Increase the Pace of Sales
   Rather Than Slow the Market"

That sure clears things up!

I wouldn't go so far as to say headlines are useless. It is always good to stay informed. However, as a predictor? Not so much.

Other headlines during early 2016:

1. "US Consumer Prices Fall on Lower Energy Prices"

    This headline appeared in many online news services on January 20, 2016, when the Consumer Price Index reportedly was down .1 percent. The lower costs of energy goods (oil and gas) were the basis for this number. This, in turn, sparked many conversations among economists on whether the Federal Reserve would see their inflation target rate of 2 percent anytime soon. Inflation is a general increase in the prices of goods and services. The biggest buzz among the economists and talking heads going into 2016 after the Fed raised the interest rates slightly in December 2015 was when and if the Fed would raise rates again, keep the status quo, or consider instituting negative rates.

2. "U.S. Consumer Spending Flat; Savings at Three-Year High"

    Retail sales (an aggregated measure of the sales of retail goods over a stated period) and consumer spending account for more than two-thirds of U.S. economic activity; it's the reason I include the Retail Sector (XRT) as a key U.S. economic sector.

Figure 10.2. Retail XRT Distribution Phase 2016 (Courtesy of Trade-Station Technologies, Inc.)

If we look at the headlines concerning the consumer, we see that Retail did in fact fall in the early part of 2016 into a Distribution Phase (figure 10.2). On January 20, the exact date that the headline about falling consumer prices appeared, XRT began to move up. Where the ellipse appears on the chart in figure 10.2 is when the price of XRT rose back above the 200-WMA and back into a Caution Phase. Is this a big surprise? No. If you look at the slope of the 200-WMA, it remains positive. That makes the Distribution Phase a weak one.

3. "January Retail Sales Rose 0.2% versus 0.1% *Increase Expected*"

This headline appeared on Bloomberg.com on February 12, 2016. Once again, figure 10.2 shows you that even before the news appeared, XRT returned over the 200-WMA. That story brought in more buyers with renewed confidence. During the next three weeks, XRT continued to gain in price. Remember, at the end of 2015 and the very beginning of 2016, economists warned of a prolonged recession. Financial planners got flooded with phone calls. Friends and family called me, panicked about their 401(k)s.

We had ample time to prepare for the worst during the Caution Phase months before. Furthermore, we had the option to buy XRT once it returned over the 200-WMA. However, since the 50-WMA had a negative slope, we could not be certain that the rally over the 200-WMA would be sustained.

As with the Russell 2000 and Real Estate charts, the crystal ball questions are: Will the slope of the overhead 50-WMA stop the rally dead in its tracks? Will the price of XRT return below the 200-WMA? Will the 50-WMA cross beneath the 200-WMA (death cross), just like it did in the Russell in 2008, thereby signaling an impending free fall?

Of course, we cannot say for sure. However, what I can guarantee you is that although headlines are useful, they are often too late or too early. Identifying phases and ascertaining how strong or weak those phases are by considering the slope of the Moving Averages will keep you much more informed and allow you to make much timelier decisions.

4. "America's 7-Year Bull Market: Can It Last?"

On March 9, 2016, this headline appeared on most online financial news services. The question is: How can we tell?

Per our definition of phases, we know that that ship has sailed (i.e., the bull market cannot last). What would make me change my mind about that? Certainly not that the market has tripled in value since its low point in 2009, indicating that the good times would never end. We know that's impossible. Phases are cyclical. They always have been and always will be. We also do not know how serious the deterioration in phases will be, going forward, or how long each phase will last.

What we do know is that, even with the charts showing a rally out of the Distribution Phase, that phase is weak because of the upward slope of the 200-WMA. We also know from the Caution Phase that the market is back and is strong, given the declining slope of the overhead 50-WMA. All we can conclude without looking at headlines is that until the slope on the 50-WMA becomes neutral to positive and the price of any instrument returns to its position above a neutral or positive sloping 50-WMA, a warning is just that: a warning and not a signal for the bulls.

Summary

1. A Distribution Phase is when the 50-WMA remains above the 200-WMA although the distance between the two MAs could be narrowing.

2. The slope on the 50-WMA usually goes from neutral to declining. The 200-WMA might also be declining in slope.

3. The price is below both the 50- and the 200-WMA.

4. Since a Distribution Phase is a movement out of investments in a particular instrument, decisions made during a Caution Phase put you well ahead of the curve.

5. During a Distribution Phase, it is normal to see the price action move up and down around the 200-WMA. Value investors come in looking for bargains. Sellers such as hedge funds, who sold during the Caution Phase or at the beginning of the Distribution Phase, begin to buy back their shares.

6. Since Distribution Phases can yield erratic price action, I wouldn't go so far as to say that headlines are useless; however, as a predictor of what may come, they are not so reliable.

CHAPTER ELEVEN
WHEN MARKETS GO LOW, HOW TO GO HIGH

The Distribution Phase can be highly volatile. As panic sets in, certain investors will surface looking to buy stocks cheaply. In fact, smart investors purposely wait for investment trusts, private investment, and mutual fund companies to panic. Once large hedge funds dump stocks, savvy investors come in and buy stocks at reduced prices.

This type of buying can translate into a rally that drives the market back up into a Caution Phase. There is a reason so many funds and individual investors wind up buying high and selling low. Clearly, these people do not understand phases. We prepared for this at the start of the Caution Phase. We know to look at the key U.S. economic sectors for early signs. We are good to go!

Every stock has to cycle through all of the phases at some point. The phase wheel goes clockwise. History has shown that completion of the circle is necessary. The amount of time that each sector or company stays in any given phase can only be determined by looking at the charts.

A Weak Distribution Phase

In a Distribution Phase that is weak (an upward slope on the 200-WMA), it's a safe bet that buyers will come back into the market or a specific instrument. During those rallies, I like to hunt for sectors of the economy that remained robust and did not experience the Distribution Phase. If I can find sectors of the economy that not only avoided a Distribution Phase but also barely entered a Caution Phase while the rest of the market sold off, that is even better.

The absolute best-case scenario is finding sectors of the economy that remained bullish during the entire time the other sectors weakened. If a stock or overall sector has "relative strength," that means it is performing stronger than the overall market.

Whether you are an investor or looking for opportunities in careers with strong companies, the best way to find opportunities is to see which areas are retaining their market value and have not budged from their strong position.

A Strong Distribution Phase

If the slope of the 200-WMA begins to neutralize or decline, however, the pressure of the overall market could eventually adversely affect even stocks that have positive relative strength. In that case, although opportunities always present themselves in other areas of the market, I prefer to prepare for more downside and not add unnecessary risk.

For opportunity seekers, downturns do indeed offer chances to make money in certain areas of the market via the "flight to safety," which is a sudden increase in appetite for safe assets such as U.S. Treasuries and cash. This refers to buying assets that are more conservative than equities, such as government securities. For those who want to protect their assets, one sector's Distribution Phase can be another sector's point to recover.

For many investors, the uncertainty of a Distribution Phase is the time when they hear from their portfolio managers that the best course of action is no course of action. After all, the stock market always improves over time, right?

Making Hay While the Sun *Don't* Shine

Finding sectors beaten up long before the rest of the market declined is equally compelling and incredibly valuable for helping folks make real-life changes while so many others run around screaming, "The sky is falling!" There are always sectors of the economy and publicly traded individual companies that have been in prolonged Bear Phases and are now ready to go countercyclical to everything else.

When I find those companies or sectors of the economy, it's like discovering the goose that lays the golden egg. Companies or sectors of the economy that awaken from a long sleep, like hibernating bears drawn out of their caves at springtime, emerge hungry. That hunger can yield incredible opportunities for those who know what to look for.

The Difference between 2008 and 2016

In 2008, after Lehman Brothers went bankrupt and homeowners began to default on their mortgages, investors very quickly withdrew about $700 billion from the stock market, and as a result, the market crashed.

A rule of thumb of investing is to diversify your investments. During other major sell-offs in the past—for example, during the tech bubble of 2000 when tech stocks plunged—other areas of the market, such as blue-chip stocks, gained. What made 2008 uniquely devastating was that almost everything fell as dramatically as the S&P 500 did.

Let's look at the chart that highlights three of the key U.S. economic sectors (Semiconductors, Biotechnology, and Transportation) plus the S&P 500 at the beginning of 2008 (figure 11.1).

Compare the broadest index or the S&P 500 to three other major sectors of the U.S. economy: Biotechnology, Transportation,

111

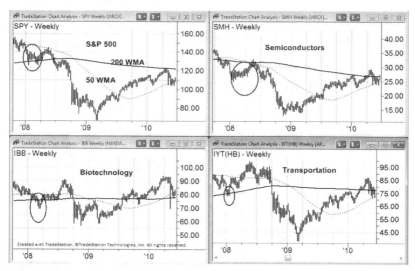

Figure 11.1. Three of the Economic Sectors Compared to the S&P 2007–2010 (Courtesy of TradeStation Technologies, Inc.)

and Semiconductors. At the start of 2008 (all highlighted with the ellipse), Semiconductors fell in price further below the 200-WMA than the other sectors did. In a strong Distribution Phase, characterized by the 50-WMA below the 200-WMA, with price under the 200-WMA and slopes on both MAs negative, a recycled fear after the 2000 bubble in the Semiconductor sector caused early panic selling. MarketGauge.com considers the relative performance of each of the major economic sectors so important that we have tools on our website that track this information.

Logically, given that these economic sectors take into account Biotechnology as the most speculated sector and not necessarily the best indicator of the U.S. economy, Biotechnology also weakened into a Distribution Phase. If you look at the S&P 500 and the Transportation sectors at the start of 2008, you'll see that both were in strong Caution Phases, but neither had really entered a Distribution Phase.

By the end of 2008, all of the four sectors plunged with the mortgage debacle. As the sector in the best shape, Biotechnology recovered first, while the S&P 500 recovered last.

How Do I Use the Phases to Make Life and Investment Decisions When I See a Sector of the Economy Outperforming the Others, Even in Hard Times?

Biotechnology was the first sector to recover, which proves my point about the Distribution Phase as a very volatile one. Not only did IBB make many speculators rich who bought companies in that sector or bought the ETF itself, but it also offered tremendous opportunities in education and in making career choices. This is a perfect example of finding the golden egg and then doing something to help your life from a place of abundance rather than fear.

Financial planners, meanwhile, suffered posttraumatic stress long after the 2008 crash. Many individuals decided to stay out of the market. A huge percentage of investors missed the greatest, most profitable, and longest-running bull market, which began in 2009–2010. Another divergence during a Distribution Phase came eight years later.

The same view of those four charts from 2014 until the first quarter of 2016 can be seen in figure 11.2.

The bull run, mentioned above, that began in certain sectors during the spring of 2009 and 2010, finally started to run out of juice in the middle to end of 2015. Once the S&P 500, Transportation, Semiconductors, and Biotechnology entered a Caution Phase (the price breaks below the 50-WMA with a negative slope), we phase watchers looking at the small caps or the Russell 2000 already knew something was up with the market. However, notice that of the four charts featured in figure 11.2, only Transportation entered a Distribution Phase at the beginning of 2016. And it was a weak one considering that the slope on the 200-WMA remained positive.

Just as the Transportation sector did, the Russell 2000, or IWM, entered a weak Distribution Phase. With a rising slope on the 200-

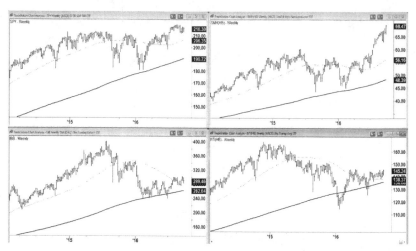

Figure 11.2. Three of the Economic Sectors Compared to the S&P 500 2014–2016 (Courtesy of TradeStation Technologies, Inc.)

WMA, the weak Distribution Phase in IWM did not last long. The eventual return in price over the 200-WMA came as no surprise given that other sectors had already returned above the 200-WMA.

For example, the S&P 500, Semiconductors, and Biotechnology all fell to their 200-WMAs, but none of them broke below that Moving Average.

When I write about the volatility that typically follows the Distribution Phase, the charts I feature here should give you a better understanding of why the market can become more volatile during that time. People are anxious, scared, and unclear as to what might be coming next.

Time to Diversify, but Should You Go to Cash?

Note the chart of the 20-Year Treasury rate from January 1994 to March 2016 in figure 11.3.

When are long-term Treasury bonds attractive to own? I personally started paying closer attention to the TLTs in 2008. At the

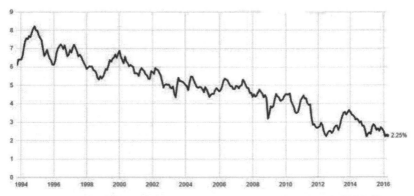

Figure 11.3. 20-Year Treasury Rate January 1994–March 2016 (Courtesy of the Board of Governors of the Federal Reserve System [US])

time, Ben Bernanke was the chairman of the Federal Reserve. It was the first time I ever heard the expression "quantitative easing" (QE).

Back in the early 1980s, when I was on the New York Commodities Exchange learning about gold, silver, sugar, oil, and the other instruments trading on the seventh floor of 4 World Trade Center, I first heard about interest rates and central banks and how they manipulated interest rates to control the then out-of-control inflation. Essentially, except for a couple of times when we refinanced our house to take advantage of lower interest rates, I barely paid attention to monetary policy. That is, until quantitative easing.

Although I had a basic knowledge and understanding about how the whole central bank, interest rate, and monetary policy thing works, with QE and the increasing role of the central banks influencing our economic lives, my goal in this next section is to simplify or modify the entire process so that we all can "get it." I am not looking to become an economist or turn you into one. Rather, I figure that since the entire process impacts the stock market, our finances, and our entire economic life, it's worth an elemental look-see.

First, a Little History and Some Definitions

In essence, quantitative easing takes place when central banks create money where there was none before. A central bank is different from a commercial bank. Commercial banks are financial institutions that offer loans to individuals and businesses, do mortgage lending, provide a place to save money, and issue checking accounts and credit cards. They also offer certificates of deposit, house safety deposit boxes, and automated teller machines, allowing you instant access to your cash twenty-four hours a day, seven days a week, anywhere in the world.

Commercial banks make profits by charging interest on money they lend and charging fees on the services they provide. Since banks rely on having many customers who deposit money with them, they must encourage people to keep their money in the bank.

Typically, banks pay you interest on the money you deposit with them. They earn that interest money by charging higher interest rates and fees to the folks who borrow money from the bank. Banks also lend to one another. If a bank has a surplus of assets, it will lend money to another bank. Called the "interbank market," this process keeps the flow of money among banks fluid.

One might ask, "What happens when banks lend to people who cannot pay them back?"

This is exactly what happened to Lehman Brothers. In 2007, after years of lending money for mortgages to people with poor credit, Lehman had no idea how many of these outstanding loans they actually had made. With a surplus of houses on the market and a growing number of people unable to pay their mortgages, Lehman Brothers, like many other banks, was no longer able to borrow money from other banks. This created a tailspin, and, as a result, banking stocks and the overall health of the stock market suffered.

Enter the Central Banks

Central banks serve as the main authority for a nation's financial affairs. The job of a central bank is to promote stability within a country's financial system. They produce and distribute currency. They implement monetary policy designed to help the country's economy grow. They then inform the public about the overall state of the economy by publishing statistics.

> A central bank is a "bankers' bank." The customers of the twelve Federal Reserve banks are not ordinary citizens but "banks" in the inclusive sense of all depository institutions—commercial banks, savings banks, savings and loan associations, and credit unions. They are eligible to hold deposits in and borrow from central banks and are subject to the "Bank" reserve requirements and other regulations.[1]

The most powerful ways that central banks have to affect monetary policy are through their ability to set interest rates and print money. To stimulate the economy, the central banks lower interest rates to encourage customers to borrow money at a lower cost. The hope is that that will increase consumer spending.

If the economy is in very bad shape, the central bank will print money. To do this, it buys government bonds (government-backed securities). A government security is a Treasury bill, bond (TLTs), or other type of debt (like a Treasury note) issued by a government.

The money the government gets from the central banks when they buy bonds and other government-backed securities gives the government room to increase spending. If the government increases spending, the hope is that it will, in turn, increase incomes. If income is increased, people spend more. If they spend more, they will also borrow more. That, in turn, helps the banks earn money in interest fees. With more credit available, the economy can turn around and go into "expansion."

In the United States, the Federal Reserve is the nation's central bank. Up until the late 1970s, the Federal Reserve and most of the global central banks "were not at the cutting edge of a market economy; they were Johnny-come-latelies."[2]

In the early 1980s, in the aftermath of the oil shocks of 1973 and 1979, when OPEC (Organization of the Petroleum Exporting

Countries) tripled the price of oil, the opposite scenario occurred. Inflation got out of control and the Federal Reserve Bank increased interest rates to make it more expensive for customers to get a loan. That led to a reduction in consumer borrowing and spending. When central banks make credit less available, the risk is that people will spend less and earn less, and without commercial banks making money from loans and deposits, the economy can spiral into a recession or worse.

In the 1980s the United States experienced brief periods of recession coupled with high unemployment. At the time, the chairman of the Federal Reserve, Paul Volcker, continued to raise interest rates regardless of the conditions, trying to break the back of the double-digit inflation rates. Then, in the 1990s, while navigating through several financial tremors such as that caused by the Gulf War, the Fed (led by Alan Greenspan) used monetary policy to raise and lower interest rates to help avert disaster.

And That Brings Us Back to Ben Bernanke, Quantitative Easing, and 2008

After the stock market crashed, in November 2008 the Federal Reserve began the first of three rounds of quantitative easing. The Fed purchased $100 billion of debt from Fannie Mae, Freddie Mac, and the federal home loan banks. (Fannie and Freddie are agencies that buy mortgages from lenders and then package those mortgages into mortgage-backed securities, which they then sell.) The Fed also bought $500 billion of those mortgage-backed securities backed by Fannie and Freddie.

Hence, the phrases "QE" and, after the Lehman Brothers debacle, "too big to fail" became part of our vernacular. By March 2009, the Fed bought $300 billion in longer-term Treasury Bonds, and in November 2010, they bought $400 billion of Treasury securities.

Then, again, in September 2012, the Fed launched QE3, which meant fresh buying of mortgage-backed securities to the tune of $40 billion per month. Two months later, they bought $45 billion per month of longer-term Treasuries.

Bernanke and the Federal Reserve did their job. Phase watchers like us saw the S&P 500 go first into a Recuperation Phase in the spring of 2009 and then, not too much later, into a Bullish Phase. After the crash of 2008, a majority of investors stayed out of the market. However, the 2009 to 2013 period will go down in history as one of the greatest bull runs of the stock market.

Furthermore, with interest rates dropping and the economy recovering, opportunities emerged in many different areas—from investing to borrowing money for buying a home to refinancing your existing home.

The ETF TLT represents the 20+ Year Treasury Bonds. This ETF holds a portfolio of Treasury Bonds that have a maturity of twenty years or longer. It reflects long-term interest-rate changes. Many investors like to trade TLTs when they desire long-term Treasury exposure. As rates drop, the TLTs rise in price.

Flight to Safety

Earlier I mentioned that downturns offer chances to make money in certain areas of the market called "flight to safety." As government debt in the United States, called "Treasury securities," is historically the safest investment during financial crises and times of uncertainty, buying U.S. debt can be a safe place to park money.

The entire case I illustrate concerning the Federal Reserve, interest rates, and how aggressively involved central banks have been since 2008 in supporting the market requires nothing more than a look at the charts to see the phases.

One thing I have learned is that historical relationships change over time. That is what I refer to as "paradigm shifts." The good news: the phases tell you when that shift is about to occur. Always check before you sell all your stocks and buy bonds!

Your 401(k), Savings, and IRAs, during a Distribution Phase—Weak and Strong 401(k) and Diversifying Assets

For a brief time in 2016, the Russell 2000 entered a Distribution Phase. That brevity and the return to the Caution Phase had everything to do with how confident investors were that the Federal Reserve along with the global central banks would continue to support the markets and world economies. Whereas the Federal Reserve and most global central banks used to be separate entities that would come in with monetary policy at a much slower pace, now they have become major players in not only the world economy but also the stock market.

Furthermore, as you look at the phases of the interest rates, particularly the TLTs versus the four stock market indices and many individual market sectors, you can start to see how they work either countercyclical to one another or in concert. That's how you can make informed decisions about savings, investing, and where to invest and where not to invest.

As Millennials enter the workforce, employers are trying to adapt to the new generation's savings and investing needs. Because many Millennials must make large monthly payments just to service their student debts, Fidelity is one company that will apply up to two thousand dollars toward the annual principal as an employment benefit. Called the Student Loan Repayment Benefit, companies like Fidelity are hoping to attract younger employees.

> Beyond Fidelity, a variety of organizations—including PricewaterhouseCoopers, Natixis Global Asset Management and Nvidia—have already either announced plans or started offering the payments. Several smaller companies—LendEDU, CommonBond, SoFi, Chegg and ChowNow—are also providing the benefit. The federal government, however, may be the pioneer here, having offered a repayment program to select employees for many years.
>
> And the list is growing. The handful of companies that administer the benefit behind the scenes—Tuition.io, Gradifi and

EdAssist among them—said demand was rising. Tim DeMello, Gradifi's chief executive, said his firm was in talks to bring about 100 more employers aboard this year, and signed 26 letters of intent.[3]

For Millennials, many of whom do prefer to have 401(k)s, some companies now match a percentage of an employee's salary contribution with the company's own contribution. If an employee contributes 5 percent of the salary, the company will put in 5 percent as well. If the company offers profit sharing to their employees as part of the 401(k) program, that pot can grow even more. I recommend you inquire about any such option where you work or would like to work. Also, inquire about whether the employer's contribution to the employee is taxable as part of your income.

How Often Should I Look at My Portfolio?

Some economists and planners advise that you look at your 401(k) once every three months. As we work with weekly charts that measure the Moving Averages for nearly one or four years, that is probably not a bad plan. Naturally, should you experience a birth, death, divorce, or loss of a job, you might need to look over the portfolio at these critical junctures in your life. If your plan is for your investments to mature over a long time, the old rule of thumb has been that stocks pay more on your initial investment than Treasury Bonds. However, since 2008, that ratio has shifted. Even though stocks have recovered from the major sell-offs in 2008 and the beginning of 2016, bonds overall have outperformed the stock market.

Like money in the bank?

It is interesting that both Keith and I come from families that did not religiously put money in a savings bank. Keith's uncle worked with Carl Icahn, Jack Dreyfus, and Carl Lindner. He went on to become a highly successful investor in the stock market. He made millions, not by saving but by focusing on what makes money. Called the "supply side," it describes the art of growing your money rather than stashing it away for a rainy day. Keith's uncle believed that saving doesn't really give anyone a chance to better their life.

My paternal grandmother bought Utilities stocks after the crash in the early 1930s. She owned shares in Con Edison, Exelon, and AT&T, to name a few. That money was passed down and never touched. When she died, we inherited some of the money. My dad added to that portfolio. Additionally, my mother discovered that she has a flair for picking value stocks (there's that consumer instinct), and currently, considering our modest background, she has a sweet cushion of investments, but, again, no real savings account.

Tony Robbins writes, "The key to success: you have to make your savings automatic."[4] Sounds so simple; yet it is not the easiest goal to accomplish. Robbins goes on to discuss "Theodore Johnson, whose first job was with the newly formed United Parcel Service in 1924." He writes that Johnson worked hard, never making more than $14,000 per year. (Considering that I was making less than that thirty years later, I imagine $14K was a handsome sum of money back in the 1920s.) Robbins states that Johnson "set aside 20% of every paycheck he received and every Christmas bonus and put it into the company stock."[5]

Now we are getting somewhere. Johnson, first off, knew to put his money in the company's stock. Either UPS had a stock plan for employees or he simply had the common sense to realize that UPS could grow and was a smart "supply side" investment. By the time Johnson was ninety years old, UPS stock had soared, yielding him more than $70 million.

Suze Orman—"Try Harder to Save"

Suze Orman's rule of thumb is simple: Money you know you need or want to spend in the next few years is for saving. Money you keep handy for an emergency belongs in savings. Money you hope to use soon for a down payment on a house belongs in savings. And all savings belong in a low-risk bank savings account or money market account. The goal is to keep your money safe so that when you go to use it, it will be there.

Money you won't need to use for at least seven years is money for investing. The goal here is to have your account grow over time to help you finance a distant goal, such as building a retirement fund. Since your goal is in the future, money for investing belongs in stocks.[6]

She's right, of course—on paper. But what happens if folks do not want to put their money in the bank because they do not collect interest? What happens when they charge you to put your money in the bank, as is happening in many places in Europe with negative interest rates?

In a zero- to negative-interest-rate environment, I suggest you learn more about the different types of bank deposit accounts offered in an FDIC (Federal Deposit Insurance Corporation) bank. If you need guidance on determining which investments or savings are best, check to see whether there is a stock or ETF symbol you can look up to see what its phase is. If you are interested in investing for yield, these are the top ETFs to track using phases. Call your investment advisor (MGAM, LLC, is ours) and review the markets with your advisor using what you have learned in this book.

Rotation: Natural Order

In math, rotation originates in geometry. It describes the motion of a rigid body around a fixed point. In the Phase Wheel chart in chapter 3 (figure 3.1), the "Big 6" is a perfect example of rotation. The six phases are like six fixed points. The actual instrument, stock, or index moves around the phases. When looking for a sector that is at a low, you are waiting for it to "rotate" into a better phase.

When searching for opportunities for investments or potential careers, look for those key U.S. economic sectors (my family) or companies that are rotating into Recuperation, Accumulation, or Bullish Phases. By doing this, you are avoiding buying or changing careers into sectors or companies that are rotating into the negative phases.

A Distribution Phase is one that suggests that worse times are coming. Therefore, the key to success is to find stocks in protracted Bear Phases that could be ready to rotate into something better.

This rotation happens constantly in the markets. I see rotation on a daily, weekly, monthly, annual, and multi-annual basis. As markets are fluid, so are phases. In fact, since we know we can depend on the rotation of phases, investors must decide whether they wish to sit through the rotation of an investment and wait for good times to return, or exit before disaster hits and then reenter when the bad times are over.

I find it fascinating to watch how the varying generations change philosophies over time. Old school is "buy and hold." Older investors believe that if you sit long enough, eventually everything comes back—and comes back stronger.

I read articles constantly that tell us to ignore warnings for the immediate future, such as a possible student-loan debt crisis, subprime auto debt issue, China debt, or fear of hyperinflation. I don't necessarily disagree, especially for those who were spooked by former negative influences in the market (i.e., the dot-com bubble). The posttraumatic stress kept them out of the market during one of the greatest rallies between 2010 and 2015.

However, I propose we pay less attention to the headlines and more attention to the phases. Furthermore, I am happy to see that the newest generation of investors, the Millennials, have become wary of the "buy and hold" philosophy and instead opt for investments to hold for five years or less.

An article titled "Wanted: Big Returns, Low Risk. (And Millennials? They Want *10.2%*)"[7] states that Millennials want a minimum of 9.1 percent annual return on their investments. Lofty, considering the average stock market return is 3.8 percent globally.

Fascinating to me is that the Millennials want this return with very little risk to their principal. Roughly 40 percent of Millennials say that they are comfortable holding assets for less than a year. Perhaps we can fine-tune that for Millennials as well. Instead of a time commitment to hold onto a stock, ETF, commodities, bonds, and so on, the phases are all they need to decide when to enter and exit! Considering that Millennials are also changing jobs at record speeds, phases are a perfect measure of time for this fast crowd.

Sector Rotation and the Key U.S. Economic Sectors

Sector rotation is a strategy based on moving investments across business *sectors* to take advantage of cyclical trends in the overall economy. The beauty of exchange-traded funds is the ease with which you can research any sector of the economy without having to navigate through hundreds of stocks. The economic sectors make that even easier for you. Instead of having to research what analysts are saying about the economy, you can look at each of the economic sectors and decide for yourself which is likely to recover or fail. When the six economic sectors are working in tandem with one another (like a happy family), confidence as a buyer should soar. If not, caution becomes your ally. And if all in the family are negative, I cannot imagine a better sign to take heed.

So, what does all that mean?

First off, take that as fair warning to reduce risk all around. If Retail, Transportation, and Regional Banks enter a more sustained Distribution Phase, then assume harder times are coming. Indeed, there are always sectors going countercyclical, and the clever investor knows how to find them. (So do you, with just a bit of research, looking at weekly charts.) Nevertheless, for most of us, how it affects our wages, savings, home values, and job security matters most. Most of the research I have done for advising folks on how to prepare for a recession sounds great on paper. For instance, increase income any way you can, get out of debt, spend nothing, and accumulate cash; unless you expect to retire within the next five years, do not sell any of your portfolio, diversify your portfolio, and so on and so on.

I have even read suggestions for more drastic preparations—buy a tent, plant seeds for food, stock up on soap and shampoo, make sure you have a couple of guns and ammo. Are you preparing for an economic downturn or Armageddon?

To keep it simple, remember this: Phases are cyclical, so, yes, the market will come back eventually. However, if (as our younger generation desires) you can shorten the life span of your investments intelligently, you do not have to panic about watching your portfolio's value get cut in half. So, yes, watch your discretionary spending. And yes, if you have an entrepreneurial spirit and can increase your income, go for it.

Where do I and many other advisors differ? While they recommend you do nothing with your portfolios, I say that is the one thing you do have power over: managing your portfolio. Yes, take steps to mitigate losses and possibly increase profits. Save money by getting out of the market or make money when the market goes down. You can make sure you are in the right asset classes, which is exactly what phases and the economic sectors help you to do.

The biggest takeaway is to avoid getting caught in a protracted bear market. Virtually every serious bear market happened because of a recession or depression. A depression is a period of severe decline in general economic activity such as financial, industrial, and employment, or a decline in real GDP beyond 10 percent and a recession that lasts more than two years.

In a serious depression, like the one beginning in 1929, it can take up to thirty years to get your money back. You want to avoid that at all costs.

Summary

1. The Distribution Phase can be volatile and, if weak, depending upon the slopes of the 50- and 200-WMAs, can bring back buyers looking for cheap equities.

2. A strong Distribution Phase is yet another warning to investors that hard times could be coming.

3. The Distribution Phase can also be an opportune time to find companies or ETFs that are ready to turn upward or go countercyclical.

4. Quantitative Easing began in 2008. It is good to check the phases of both interest rates and the dollar before making decisions on going to cash, borrowing money, and diversifying your portfolio.

5. The economic sectors are the six ETFs that best represent the U.S. economy. Rotation of those ETFs tells you everything you need to know about how safe or risky major stock investments are at any given phase.

CHAPTER TWELVE

THE BEARISH PHASE—DESPAIR

Back on September 15, 2008, we were sitting in our friend's guest villa in Tuscany; we had the television on CNN because we knew about the subprime crisis and particularly that Lehman Brothers had declared bankruptcy.

With saucer-wide eyes, we watched the Dow Jones melt down that day 504.48 points. We spent two weeks in Italy with our friends, and on September 29, while dunking biscotti into our cups of cappuccino, we watched the Dow drop another 778 points. By the end of October, the market plummeted another 13 percent. At the conclusion of 2008, the Dow dropped a whopping 34 percent for the year.

We saw the S&P 500 first enter a Caution Phase in late 2007, followed by a Distribution Phase in the summer of 2008. We were entirely out of the market long before the collapse. I like to use 2008 as a prime example of when heightened selling pressure ensues. As a "head for the exits" year, 2008 serves as the quintessential example of a Bear Phase.

"The Bearish Phase is evidence of a complete lack of demand, and of supply overwhelming what little demand there is."[1]

When buyers have disappeared from the market, leaving only the sellers, most sellers find themselves panicking. With no one to sell to, prices fall harder and faster. Oftentimes, the public exits long positions at the absolute lows. Part of the reason is the overriding philosophy of many financial planners and hedge fund operators that one should never sell their stocks. The danger in that is they wait and wait to sell until panic takes over.

How Do I Identify a Bearish Phase?

1. The 50-WMA (dotted line) (figure 12.1) is below the 200-WMA (solid line).

2. The slope on the 50-WMA is negative. The slope on the 200-WMA has neutralized and is starting to turn negative.

3. The price or cost in dollars is now below both the 50- and the 200-WMA.

The S&P 500 (SPY) chart in figure 12.1 shows the progression in 2008 from a Caution to Distribution and ultimately into the Bearish Phase. The point where the 50-WMA crosses beneath the 200-WMA is aptly called a "death cross."

You can see that by the time SPY entered a death cross in October 2008, a lot of damage had been done. The price of where the Moving Averages crisscrossed (around 130) versus the actual price SPY was trading at (90–100) did not offer any new buyers or sellers an advantage. Ideally, if you are looking to make a trade, you want to see the price as close to the Moving Averages as possible. Why? To control risk.

If you look back to the beginning of 2008, when the S&P 500 entered a Caution Phase, the price sat right on the 50-WMA. That told us that the market was in trouble long before we visited our friend's villa in Italy in September that year. Furthermore, we had a very low-risk opportunity to go short.

Figure 12.1. The S&P 500 Bearish Phase 2007–2009 (Courtesy of TradeStation Technologies, Inc.)

SPY broke down first. Considering the companies that had the worst issues later that year—AIG, Lehman Brothers, and Bear Stearns—those Fortune 500 companies had to affect the rest of the U.S. economy.

On October 3, 2008, the Russell 2000 (IWM) opened up lower than the closing price from the day before. I call that a gift. If short sellers turned out to be wrong, they would have known immediately. Why? The price would have returned above the two Moving Averages. That did not happen. The IWM dropped from seventy dollars down to thirty-five dollars by March 2009.

If you look at a chart of the Russell 2000 from 2008, you will see that the slopes on both the 50- and the 200-WMA were negative. These differences in how and when different instruments break down or break out are important to note. It helps you figure out the leaders and the laggards. It trains you to look at the merits of individual sectors of the economy. It helps you make wiser and timelier decisions for you and your family.

The financial crisis of 2008 was the worst recession since the Great Depression. The history books consider the start date of the recession to be December 2007, with the end date June 2009.

Knowing how to identify phases on these weekly charts empowers us to see recessions and recoveries easily, often even well before the economists write the history books.

Another Bear Phase at Another Time

The S&P 500 (SPY) was the first ETF introduced to the United States. It began trading in 1993. An interesting digression: Kathleen Moriarty, a lawyer in New York, helped launch SPY. To this day, Ms. Moriarty continues to lead the way in taking on the Securities and Exchange Commission authorities so that new ETFs may continue to emerge. The NASDAQ 100 (QQQ) began trading in 1999.

In order to see Weekly Moving Averages on these charts, we need at least fifty weeks or one year of data. Therefore, the S&P 500 (SPY) is the best ETF we have to illustrate another Bear Phase that occurred in the twenty-first century. Incidentally, none of our key U.S. economic sectors has ETFs going back nearly as far. Real Estate (IYR) was the first sector ETF introduced in June 2000.

At the end of 2000, the S&P 500 (SPY) went into a Caution Phase. The slope on the 50-WMA turned negative. Then, by the fall of 2001, a death cross occurred. Although the slope on the 200-WMA stayed neutral, by the summer of 2002, it turned negative. Similar to the SPY chart from 2007, the better time to head for the hills or go short the market was at the start of the Caution Phase. Slope, price, and the phase should all line up.

By the time SPY entered the Bear Phase in mid-2001, the price dropped too far from the Moving Averages for a low-risk short trade. What it does illustrate, however, is the continued selling by the panicked mutual fund managers afraid of losing their jobs.

By the spring of 2003, the worst was over. You can always bank on hopefulness and a better time returning to the market. It's human nature. Now, you can track better times coming by using the phase changes.

The Major Headlines of 2000–2003

The headline that trumps all other headlines reports the attacks of September 11, 2001. Interestingly, the market had already been declining, as mentioned, starting in October 2000. By the time 9/11 happened, the stock market took a brief dive, only to turn back up. However, it could not clear the 50-WMA on that pop. Further declines ensued in 2002.

The events of 9/11 profoundly touched everyone in one way or another. Personally, after working in the World Trade Center for twelve years, I watched in horror as the buildings fell. Although neither of us worked there in 2001, my husband, Keith, had planned to go to the Water Technology Conference for leading Wall Street technologists that day. Participants were meeting at 9 a.m. in Windows on the World, the restaurant on the top floor of the World Trade Center. Scheduled to attend with his friend Ari Jacobs, at the last minute Keith decided not to go, as he had an unscheduled, yet pressing, business matter. Ari and nearly three thousand others tragically lost their lives that day.

Long before the 9/11 attacks, the U.S. economy began a major slowdown in the manufacturing sector. Here are the top economic stories from that period:

Headlines—2001

1. From 1997 until its peak, occurring on March 10, 2000, the dot-com bubble occurred. SPY went into a Bullish Phase before the Warning Phase in October 2001. With the rapid growth of the internet, speculators poured into stocks. Companies like Amazon saw their stock go from $107 down to $7 per share. From March 11, 2000, until

October 9, 2002, the NASDAQ Composite lost 78 percent of its value.

2. On October 25, 2001, the House passed a $100 billion economic stimulus package. That announcement coincides with a pop after 9/11. However, by the spring of 2002, it wasn't enough to help the market sustain that pop.

Headlines—2002

3. Enter Enron, Merrill Lynch, and a host of other companies that took heat over allegations of corruption. Furthermore, a corporate-reform bill passed: Enron, Arthur Andersen, Tyco, Qwest, Global Crossing, ImClone, and Adelphia, among others, were convicted of obstruction of justice or placed under federal investigation. In 2005, the Supreme Court overturned Andersen's conviction, citing the jury's failure to "convey the requisite consciousness of wrong-doing." Nonetheless, the damage to the stock market was done.

Headlines—2003

4. The War in Iraq and the capture/death of Saddam Hussein. The U.S.-led coalition on March 19 (the beginning of the Iraq War) coincides with the return of SPY over the 50-WMA.

A Spectacular Bear Phase with a Double-Edged Impact

The trouble in the oil market began in 2011. Well, really it began in 2008 when everything crashed. The 50- and 200-WMAs do not go back far enough to show you, as USO (United States Oil Fund) is a relatively new energy-based ETF. However, suffice to say that for some, the best news has been cheap oil. From a phase point of view, USO has not traded in a Bullish Phase since the early part of 2007. Yet the chart in figure 12.2 shows a series of fits and starts where the 50-WMA crosses both above and below the 200-WMA several times.

How do we ascertain a strong or weak golden or death cross? The best way I know is by looking at the slopes of both MAs. When 2012 began, USO sat above the 50-WMA and below the 200-WMA. That is a Recuperation Phase. Prior to that, at the end of 2011, USO was in a Bear Phase. Although the slope was clearly negative during that entire period on the 200-WMA, the 50-WMA had a more neutral to slightly negative slope.

Phase changes when the slope is not in line with the phase (i.e., a negative slope in the 50-WMA during a Recuperation Phase) are not a strong signal to be a buyer. Although I would not sell in a Recuperation Phase, I would not buy in a weak one, either. I prefer to wait for the next sell signal, assuming that the rally was bottom pickers. We did not have to wait too long. In April 2012, USO's price fell below the 50-WMA. By late September 2012, USO had a death cross and entered a Bearish Phase.

Figure 12.2. U.S. Oil Fund Bearish Phase 2012–2016 (Courtesy of TradeStation Technologies, Inc.)

Notice, though, the slope on the 200-WMA during that time. It flattened. Although USO eventually dropped significantly, the activity until that point was erratic. The slopes changed on both WMAs several times until August 2014. At that point, the sell-off and Bear Phase gained tremendous momentum.

It is common to see erratic phase changes before the start of a much more prolonged move. For traders, this usually means to avoid trading that instrument. For phase watchers, it can help you "stay the course" until the phase gains momentum in one direction or another.

Summary

1. The Bearish Phase is when the 50-WMA crosses below the 200-WMA. This is a death cross. The price, or dollar amount, is below both WMAs.

2. The slope on both the 50- and the 200-WMA should be declining. The more the decline, the greater the momentum of the Bear Phase.

3. The Bearish Phase follows the Distribution Phase after a period of redistribution of cash and a lack of buyers. Expect to see headlines that reflect a somber mood both economically and geopolitically.

4. When a Bear Phase wavers from Bearish to Recuperation and back to Bearish, check the slopes on the two Weekly Moving Averages. A good time to demonstrate patience, it is best to wait for momentum and a sustained move with negative slopes before trading or making any life-changing decisions. Erratic trading or price movements during a phase change usually mean a much bigger move is coming.

CHAPTER THIRTEEN
FINDING OPPORTUNITIES WHEN TIMES ARE TOUGH

No doubt, Bearish Phases can get nasty. However, they provide opportunities. With that said, a true bear market is not a correction. We must remember that widespread pessimism and negative sentiment in a bear market can last for many months, years, or decades. Japan's stock market (Nikkei 225) peaked in 1989 at 38,915.87. At the midpoint of 2018, it was still trading at 40 percent less than at its peak.

Timing the bottom of a bear market is not our concern. We have recognizable phases that tell us when the bottom is reached. Furthermore, preparing for a Bear Phase can happen long before it even occurs. Caution and Distribution Phases are the harbingers of a Bear Phase. Moreover, you can bank on the fact that, even as conditions improve during the Caution and Distribution Phases, eventually all cycles must end. A Bear Phase *will* come to a theater near you. Like life and death, it is inevitable.

Panic

Large sell-offs happen as a Bearish Phase gains in momentum. How do we know momentum is accelerating? The slopes on the 50- and 200-WMAs decline precipitously. Generally, right before a Bear Phase or in the beginning of a Bear Phase, investors come into the market to "bargain shop." Very often, these investors are mutual fund managers who only make commissions when they buy. Naturally, once they see that the market cannot recover and begin to experience deep losses, they panic.

Good Times and Bad Times: What You Need to Know about Mutual Fund Managers

Mutual fund managers mainly get paid on performance. Here's the tricky part. One measures the performance of the stock(s) a manager is holding against the performance of the index the stock trades in. For example, if a portfolio manager bought Facebook (stock symbol FB), then you measure the performance of that stock against how NASDAQ is doing.

If Facebook is down 3 percent for the year and NASDAQ is up 1 percent, then the portfolio manager is underperforming. That means the portfolio manager may have to sell that stock. Otherwise, he might lose his job or his bonus if he continues to underperform NASDAQ or the "benchmark" (the corresponding index the instrument is in).

How Does This Relate to a Bearish Phase?

In a Bearish Phase, professional traders can short sell a stock (sell stock anticipating the price will go lower), while portfolio mutual fund managers cannot, because short selling is when you sell a security or stock you do not own. Fund managers only get paid to own stocks and by law are not allowed to short stocks.

During significant Bearish Phases like the ones in 2001 and 2008, mutual fund portfolio managers quickly sold stocks that were underperforming their benchmarks. Liquidating these bad positions in hopes of saving their jobs only fuels the decline even further.

Professional traders know and count on funds panicking during vicious Bearish Phases. Therefore, short sellers become aggressive.

As they become aggressive, fund managers are even more unwilling to buy. They do not want losers in their portfolio. Since fund managers only get paid to own stocks, they sit and wait before reentering the market. Hence, demand for stocks shrinks further during prolonged Bear Phases.

Eventually, the selling dries up, and buyers come back in. Typically, the first ones to buy are the professionals. Mutual fund managers often miss the best opportunity to buy any stock or index with the lowest amount of risk. The deep losses they probably just took leave them feeling tentative and anxious.

Phase watchers—you do not have to be that hamster on a wheel. You can sell before the dump and buy before the fund managers do! In essence, you, too, can invest like a professional.

In this situation you might wonder, "Should I play dead?"

If you cannot trust the portfolio and fund managers and do not know how to (or even want to) sell short stocks, then playing dead is an old adage to follow. Considering that most Bear Phases are defined by stock market declines of 20 percent or more, playing dead often means selling out all stocks and going to cash.

That was then, and this is now.

Since 2008, the term "going to cash" during Bear Phases has meant saving on losses in the market. However, it does not mean earning interest at the bank. Therefore, your money is playing dead. That may not be the worst thing while the market goes through a big decline. However, take note: Interest rates near zero mean that your money is not growing at the bank. It's a repository and nothing more.

The Relationship of the U.S. Dollar and a Bear Phase

The chart in figure 13.1 is of the U.S. Dollar Index (DXY). It shows the value of the U.S. dollar relative to a basket of foreign currencies. The euro has the most weight in that basket, making up 57.6

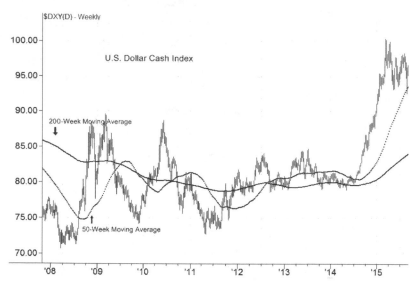

Figure 13.1. The U.S. Dollar 2007–2016 (Courtesy of TradeStation Technologies, Inc.)

percent of the DXY index. If the DXY price rises, it shows that there is strength in the U.S. dollar.

In order to purchase U.S. stocks, you need to pay in dollars. Therefore, typically if the stock market is going up, so should the dollar. Both are increasing in value.

Wait a minute.

Although there are formulas that analysts use to figure out the correlation between the dollar and the market, they only work about 50 percent of the time. Charts, and particularly identifying phases, are what I consider the most reliable, as the correlation between the U.S. dollar (DXY) and the S&P 500 (SPY) changes from positive to an inverse correlation.

In 2008–2009, the dollar rose in value. As interest rates dropped close to zero, global investors borrowed dollars to buy stocks and commodities. The financial crisis around the world made the dollar more attractive than other currencies. You might see a rising market and a rising dollar when the economy is in strong shape. Otherwise, it is hard to predict the relationship between the two.

Had you gone to cash in 2008 during that spectacular Bear Phase in the market, your dollar would have increased in value.

2000–2003

A very different scenario occurred in 2000. The stock market went into a Bear Phase, and by mid-2002, so did the U.S. dollar. Had you gone into all cash at that time, no doubt there was safety in that, but your dollars lost value.

Was 2000–2003 Considered a Recession?

A recession, by definition, is when the United States experiences two consecutive quarters of negative growth or a negative gross domestic product. During the period of 2000–2003, the United States had only one period of negative growth. The market declined more seriously after the 9/11 attacks, and the dollar remained steady.

Then, as the U.S. market continued to decline, so did the dollars because the economic picture changed. The unemployment statistics rose from 4.2 percent in February 2001 to 5.5 percent in November 2001 and then continued to rise, with a temporary top at 6.3 percent in June 2003.

2012–2018 Economic Growth

The U.S. economy gained in strength as the unemployment numbers began to drop from their peak at 9.9 percent posted in April 2010. By the start of 2015, unemployment dropped to 5.7 percent. To date, the lowest number since the 2010 peak was 3.8 percent in May 2018. In addition to a rising U.S. stock market, you had a rising U.S. dollar. All this while interest rates continued to stay at or near zero percent.

The ever-changing relationships can make the best economists' heads spin. For us laypeople, the takeaway is that during market crashes, it is generally a good idea to run into safety with bonds or cash. However, it is equally empowering to know whether your dollars will buy you more or less. And if you put those hard-earned dollars in the bank, it is good to know how much interest (if any) you will collect.

Another point to consider is that there is no hard-and-fast rule for how interest rates, the dollar, and the stock market all correlate with one another. Having these basic weekly charts to decipher and make your own best decisions is the best way I know to give you a better handle on your money and finances.

Then there is Oil and Gas.

Continuous Contract in Oil and Other Futures

Although currently more and more commodity futures have a corresponding exchange-traded fund (ETF) for traders to invest in, the continuous contract is helpful to look at if one wants to see historical price action. Simply put, the whole idea of "futures" trading began so that farmers could hedge against how their crop might do by buying or selling contracts on the commodities or futures exchanges.

If a farmer who grows corn has 5,000 bushels to sell, he has two choices: He can sell to a local wholesaler (grain operator), or he might sell (go short) in the corn futures market for a later date and lock in his price. That way, the farmer preserves the value of his 5,000 bushels. If the price per bushel should fall by the time he sells his corn, the price on the futures market will also fall. The farmer then buys the corn back, delivers it, or covers the short of his corn futures at a lower price.

Likewise, speculators who have no interest in growing corn will also buy and sell the futures. Speculators buy and sell futures based on what they expect the price to be in the future for a crop or any other commodity. If the weather forecast is for drought conditions, you will see speculators and farmers buy corn in the futures market, expecting to see the price rise in the future.

Buying a stock in a company means owning a piece of that company. If the company does well and the stock goes up in price, you make a profit. Selling a stock in a company means betting against that company or, in essence, believing that the company's stock price will fall. Buying a sector exchange-traded fund such as retail (XRT) means you are buying into a basket of different retail companies.

Commodities are not companies from which you can profit share. They are raw materials. Buying a future means speculating that the price of that commodity will rise by a certain month. Futures trade month by month. You can buy a future for the following month or you can buy as far out as twelve months or more in the future. If buying December corn, you have until December to see the price of corn rise. Once that month is over, the contract of corn will expire. Many traders will sell out before the month expires and roll out or buy the next month.

Figure 13.2 is a continuous contract chart. It shows you a continuing price without having an expiration date for each month.

Figure 13.2. Continuous Contract Crude Oil 2008–2016 (Courtesy of TradeStation Technologies, Inc.)

This particular continuous chart of oil shows price action over years by splicing when one contract expires and another one begins. Although not spliced together in a way that shows an entirely smooth price transition, it is close enough for us to see the phases in oil since 2008.

Looking at Ellipse A, you can see that after a sharp move higher in oil at the beginning of 2008, the price crashed fast and hard. "A" is where oil went from a Bullish to a Caution Phase. As the price declined, so did the slope on the 50-WMA. In the beginning of 2009, although oil recovered in price and the slope on the 50-WMA neutralized, the price did not return over the 200-WMA. Furthermore, the slope on the 200-WMA remained negative, even as the chart ended in the middle of 2016.

Ellipse B shows the death cross or start of the Bearish Phase in oil in 2009. From 2009 until the end of 2014, the price of oil on the continuous contract did not move up or down significantly. The price remained between $90 and $120 per barrel. The phases changed frequently from Recuperation to Accumulation, briefly back to Bullish in 2013 and 2014, and then back to Bearish by the end of 2015. It remained in a Bearish Phase as of November 2016. The slopes on both the 50- and the 200-WMA are negative.

Ellipse C, at the end of November 2016, indicates that a change might be coming for the price of oil. Since 2008, oil prices have been very low, so it appears that the phase could change to a Recuperation Phase.

What Do Cheap Oil and Gas Prices Mean?

We all love to go to the pumps and fill our tank with inexpensive gas. I have a Range Rover. Yes, living in Santa Fe has helped us limit our carbon footprint. Nevertheless, even though I fill up a lot less than I used to when we lived in New York, the savings since gas prices fell have been substantial. In 2016, instead of costing seventy-five to one hundred dollars to fill up the twenty-three-gallon tank, it cost thirty-five to fifty-five dollars. Lower oil prices have some real benefits. They also have some real consequences.

Benefits

A drop in fuel prices means lower transportation costs. Booking cheaper airline tickets promotes travel. That in turn boosts hotel, restaurant, airline, and cruise line businesses. If you are interested in buying stocks that benefit from a period of declining oil prices, the travel and restaurant businesses are good places to look. Now that you know how to distinguish a positive from a negative phase, I advise you to look only at businesses in Recuperation, Accumulation, and/or Bullish Phases.

If you live in a cold climate or drive a considerable distance to work each day, lower oil prices help you save a decent amount of money. Ironically, nearly 40 percent of American families that earn $40,000 per year or less did not typically profit from the bull run in the stock market between 2012 and 2015. Yet those families wind up with the advantage when oil prices are down. In a time when wages have barely budged upward, many families can save significant money when heating oil for their homes or gas for their cars costs less.

Cheap gas, which is expected to persist due to a global slowdown in demand for energy, saved American households around $65 billion in just the first half of 2015, according to the American Automobile Association (AAA). For the year, savings should exceed $100 billion, or more than $750 per household, according to economists at IHS Global Insight. The U.S. Energy Information Administration forecasts gasoline prices will remain under three dollars a gallon at least through the end of next year, which would be the longest such stretch since prices plunged during the recession.[1]

Disadvantages

Since 2014 and in spite of lower gasoline prices, consumer spending has not increased as much as economists would expect.

Perhaps the best way to see how little impact lower gas prices have had on overall consumer spending is by looking at our "Grandmother of Retail" (XRT) and the Retail ETF.

Looking back at the continuous contract chart of crude oil (figure 13.2), you can see that between 2010 and the big crash at the end of 2015, oil prices were trading relatively sideways. At the same time, retail spending rose precipitously. Interestingly, once oil prices declined in the fall of 2015, the relationship of cheaper oil increasing consumer spending changed to cheaper oil decreasing consumer spending. By the final quarter of 2015, XRT went into a Caution Phase. At the beginning of 2016, XRT entered a Distribution Phase.

Although Retail improved in early spring 2016, by the end of May, XRT fell back below the 200-WMA and back into a Distribution Phase. Furthermore, we can gather that economists are not "gurus," as paradigms and historical relationships change. Finally, phase-change watchers get a shout-out, as now we know how to monitor our financial decisions independently from the "experts."

The conclusions one can draw when oil prices drop and consumer spending declines are:

1. Oil could rise in price again.

2. The global and U.S. sectors that depend on higher oil prices could affect overall economic growth in the United States.

3. Consumers, although saving some money, are still not convinced they should spend more money.

4. Regardless of what oil prices do next, consumers are wary of a possible economic downturn and so tighten their belts. Hence, this is not a good time to invest in retail stocks.

5. It is time to watch the Retail sector chart for signs of a death cross or entry into a Bearish Phase.

6. It behooves you to watch how the U.S. dollar fares at all times. Although investing in retail may not be wise, saving money is not yielding very much either. If the dollar rises in value while oil prices are cheap, then at least the money we save from lower gas prices stretches further to buy the things we do need.

7. Once oil prices rise, continue to watch the dollar, interest rates, and the economic sectors. These can help determine whether the economy is pointing toward more recovery, inflation, recession, or worse, stagflation (when the dollar decreases in value, inflation rises fast, and the economy slows down).

When making smart financial and life decisions during a Bear Phase, it's important to watch the charts related to the job you have.

If you work for a company dependent upon making money in the oil and gas industry, watch the charts in those sectors. That could give you a jump start on trying to find out whether your job is secure or, possibly, on determining the timing of finding yourself a new job.

In the first three months of 2016, the U.S. oil industry cut more than 23,200 jobs. That makes the total job cuts since the beginning of 2015 nearly 118,000. Worldwide, the estimated job cuts in the oil industry are around 342,000, to date.

Looking back at the continuous contract in oil chart (figure 13.2), we see that it went into a strong Caution Phase in 2008–2009. Eight years later, those who knew how to watch phases and make decisions accordingly potentially had the opportunity to avert financial hardship.

Your Retirement Account

Learning about phases and what to do (or not do) during each phase, you can hopefully make intelligent changes to your 401(k) or IRA accounts during a Caution or Distribution Phase, so by the time the Bear Phase hits, you're not panicking.

Since the whole idea of understanding phase changes relates to how much risk one should have at any given time, the rule of thumb is to decrease your risk capital during bad times and increase it during boom times.

For example, now that you have met Grandma Retail or the ETF XRT, any stocks in her wheelhouse that are beginning to decline are not good to sit with during deteriorating phases. It is time to sell those stocks.

If by the time a Bear Phase is in the works you are already out of a lot of risky stocks and into cash, bonds, or other asset classes that are outperforming, there is no need to do anything. In fact, you are in great shape. This is the time to sit and wait for the Bear move to taper off. Now start to look for investments that are beginning to go into our next phase—the Recuperation Phase. Until then, you can comfortably ride out the storm.

Statistically, people who have the wherewithal to exit or sell stocks before a bear market become too frightened to get back in when the market begins to rebound. Personally, I am most excited during a bear market, especially a prolonged one, because I can smell opportunity afoot.

Without understanding how phases work, even the professional fund managers tend to buy high and sell low. Watching the phases transition long before they get to Bullish or Bearish stages is not 100 percent effective, but it is darn close.

Opportunities in Stocks Recovering or Going Countercyclical

The expression "One man's trash is another man's treasure" originated in the seventeenth century. The English proverb stated, "One man's meat is another man's poison." What is worthless to one investor may be valuable to another. It is in that spirit that I find my sweet spot for opportunities well ahead of the curve.

3-D Printing

For several years now, news stories have appeared about the advancements made in 3-D printing. Jeremy Rifkin, an American economist, social theorist, and political advisor, wrote a book called *The Third Industrial Revolution* in 2011.[2] He believes, as do I, that 3-D printing is at the forefront of a third industrial revolution. Some analysts predict that the "3-D printing market could grow from $4B in 2014 to up to $490B by 2025."[3]

Currently, 3-D printing has a plethora of functions in the industrial realm—from aerospace to architecture to medical replacements, just to name a few. For consumers, many companies are attempting to make affordable 3-D printers for home use. Naturally, as with all technological advancements, there are pros and cons for social change. Nevertheless, 3-D printing is here and will undoubtedly decrease the impact of manual labor in our society to one more focused on digital technology.

The chart in figure 13.3 is for 3D Systems Corporation (DDD). The company engineers, manufactures, and sells 3-D printers.

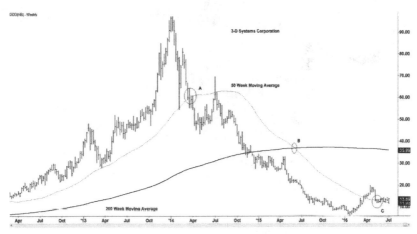

Figure 13.3. 3–D Printing 2012–2016 (Courtesy of TradeStation Technologies, Inc.)

Throughout 2013 up until its peak in 2014, DDD was in a strong Bullish Phase. Then, as the price began to drop (Ellipse A), DDD fell under the 50-WMA. Thus began its Caution Phase.

Typical of the end of a long-term trend up and into Caution, the price did not drop right away. In previous chapters, I mentioned that prices can fluctuate between phases, especially when a prolonged phase is about to end. By the time you see Ellipse B, or the death cross and entry into a Bear Phase, DDD has had a significant drop in price. Note the slope on the 50-WMA. It also declined sharply. Now note the slope on the 200-WMA. That took much longer to neutralize and then, eventually, gently turned downward.

During the price decline, DDD had disappointing earnings and some operational challenges. With declining sales and increasing competition, DDD remained in a Bear Phase until Ellipse C, which shows the price returning above the 50-WMA.

Although the slope on the 50-WMA remains slightly negative, this chart exemplifies a relatively prolonged Bear Phase in a company that had done a lot better a few years before. Furthermore, 3-D printing is an industry that has real long-term growth potential.

For investors taking a chance, buying a stock like DDD offers a low-risk opportunity. All longer-term investors need to do is watch the 50-WMA. If the price falls below, investors can take a relatively small loss. If the slope turns up, investors can buy more of the stock.

For the purposes of studying phases and looking for companies already in a Bear Phase with the potential to improve, DDD makes a fine example.

On July 19, 2016, the 3-D Printing ETF, called PRNT, launched for trading. With more than fifty companies in this ETF's basket, 3D Systems Corporation ranks first. The recent issue date of PRNT does not yet provide enough back data to allow us to see any Weekly Moving Averages, but you can at least watch this instrument going forward.

Using the Bear Phase to Make Career Choices

No doubt, when the market tumbles into a Bear Phase, folks have reasons to feel scared. Now that you can check a weekly chart on the company you work for or want to work for (if it is a publicly traded one), seeing your company's stock price tank into a Bear Phase will cause alarm.

What happens if your company does not enter a Bear Phase when the rest of the stock market does? That could be great news. That could also be a warning that if the economy goes into a tailspin or the market continues to decline, your company may still enter a Bear Phase. What phase is your company in? Caution? Distribution? Either way, it might be a good time for you to assess, as best you can, the future of the company where you work.

Furthermore, knowing which sector of the economy the company you work for is in would be helpful information. For example, if you work for an oil company, what phase is the oil sector in? If your company is a publicly traded company, what phase is your company in?

The chart in figure 13.4 shows each week in XOP, the ETF that represents oil and gas exploration. In the ellipse, you can see the huge decline, not only in price but also in the deterioration of phases from Caution to Bearish. This industry has taken a big hit in the United States and in other countries that rely on oil and gas to support their economies.

If you work in the oil and gas industry, you might have received a layoff notice. However, before the bulk of layoffs began in the United States in 2015, the chart in figure 13.4 illustrates that the industry entered a strong Caution Phase in the fall of 2014. Of course, hindsight is 20/20. However, looking at the phase of the industry you work in or plan to work in can definitely help you make educated choices.

What Might You Do to Protect Yourself?

First, have faith that the best part of a Bear Phase is that it eventually ends. Therefore, whatever contingency plans you make

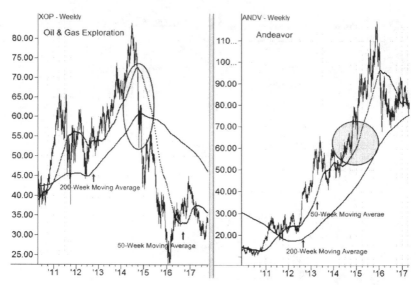

Figure 13.4. Oil and Gas Exploration (XOP) 2010–2016/Andeavor (ANDV) 2011–2016 (Courtesy of TradeStation Technologies, Inc.)

for yourself and your family, you can at least take some solace in knowing that the downturn might not last more than two years. That means once you see a chart of your industry or company go into a Caution Phase, you have time to take some steps to protect yourself before things deteriorate.

Tips for Preparing for Hard Times

1. If your company is in the gas or oil industry, check to see whether it is a publicly traded stock. If your company has entered a Caution Phase, you might consider talking to your boss to see whether he or she is privy to any discussions about the future. Have they met with the higher-ups and been warned of budget and/or job cuts? It's possible your boss will not know the answers to those questions, but at least you have made him or her aware. That could also add to your value as an employee. You've

just shown your boss you are on the ball. Maybe even show him or her a chart. Maybe buy him or her a copy of this book!

2. If you have been living beyond your means up to the point of seeing a shift in phase, definitely cut back expenditures (if possible). Lowering the interest rate on credit cards and reducing the amount of money owed is not that hard to do if you take the necessary time. Furthermore, check the interest rates for a home equity loan. With the interest rates historically low since 2008, it's possible that a loan can help you pay off credit card debt and also give you some emergency cash should you need it.

3. We have already discussed how to manage your retirement accounts (if applicable). Moreover, with the ETFs I have shown you throughout the book, you could open up a small trading account and consider selling an ETF that is beginning to deteriorate in phase. MarketGauge .com specializes in teaching you about how to take the least amount of risk and how to manage your risk once you have made a trade.

4. There are also specific formulas for when to take profits. Even a small trading account, managed well, can yield extra money. So, as perverse as it might seem to "short" (sell stock anticipating the price will go lower) the industry you work in, it is actually the American way! Hedging against hard times goes back to the 1800s when farmers bought and sold "futures of corn" in case they had a bad or a banner crop. If you look again at the XOP chart in figure 13.4, notice that where the chart ends in June 2016, the price crossed back over the 50-WMA. That Recuperation Phase is your signal that the worst has passed. It is also a good time to think about buying back

any "short" position and maybe going "long" (buying stock) now that you have made money in the market!

5. In previous chapters, I mentioned that not all companies in any particular industry are necessarily doing as poorly or as well as many other companies might be doing. That's where a modicum of research can be hugely helpful to you. Perhaps it's time to consider applying for a job in a similar company that is doing better than yours.

Go to http://www.etf.com/XOP[4] for everything you need to know about any ETF. In this case, XOP—the Oil and Gas Exploration ETF page—has lots of information. The information you need is available if you scroll down the page. There you will find "XOP Top 10 Countries." Interestingly, 100 percent of this ETF is in the United States. Beneath that, you will see the "XOP Top 10 Holdings." If you click on "View All," you get a list of every company that is part of the XOP ETF. The percentage listed beside the company's name indicates how weighted that company is in the ETF.

I literally checked every company's stock and its weekly chart. Look what I found: Marathon Petroleum (MPC), formerly known as Andeavor and, before that, the Tesoro Corporation! Before I even looked into where the company is located, how many employees it has, and so on, I checked the phase the stock was trading in. Now remember, at the end of 2014, XOP began its descent into a Caution Phase. In figure 13.4 I highlight with an ellipse the phase where MPC is. What have you learned so far? This phase is *Bullish*! The slopes on both the 50- and the 200-WMA are pointing up! So I look into the company's website, http://www.andeavor.com/. I click on "Careers."

Here's what I read:

To explore opportunities to accelerate or refine your career at Marathon Petroleum, register with our Career Center and create a career profile and online resume today. Through your career profile, you can search for opportunities, apply for multiple positions and set-up notification alerts for when positions of interest become available. Our recruiters will also use the information you provide to match our talent needs with your skills, expertise and experience.

We invite you to grow with Marathon and look forward to hearing from you!

I found out that Andeavor is headquartered in San Antonio, Texas, and has more than 3,300 retail locations in seventeen states throughout the United States. If I were you, I'd be filling out an application!

I Own My Company; What Should I Do?

If you own a company, it could be a good time to recruit top-shelf employees that other companies laid off and are looking for new jobs.

As many excellent candidates may have lost their jobs during a recession or prolonged Bear Phase, this can become a great time to look for talent. According to many recruiters or headhunters, there is a twelve- to eighteen-month window of opportunity for employers to hire the top 25 percent of employees who might be searching for jobs. Recruiters further recommend employers ensure that they have a great hiring process so that they can separate the average applicants from the superior ones.

Another tip is to use a bear market as a time to upgrade your existing team. Experts say that employers should assess whether the existing team is merely average or doing all they should be doing. If anyone on your team falls below expectations, the recession and the gift of a job pool of the best candidates is advantageous.

Address other concerns during a downturn by expanding sales of new products and/or using the time to come up with new products to sell. Ideas include considering entering new markets through affiliates, partnerships, or acquisitions. You can also consider a franchise or merger.

Furthermore, to ensure you don't run out of capital, try to increase a line of credit or establish new lines of credit. You should also evaluate your credit terms with other vendors to see whether you are paying your creditors too soon compared to the competition. If applicable, you can consider outsourcing anything not strategic to your business. Payroll, accounting, and manufacturing outsourced could save your company a lot of money. If you own the real estate your business operates from, take advantage of the hard times by reinvesting that real estate capital into something more profitable.

The key is to empower your decision making well ahead of time by using the phases to get and be prepared. Long before the economy goes into a tailspin, seeing the phase turn down into Caution is your signal to start protecting your business from financial ruin or bankruptcy!

Is This a Good Time to Consider Starting Your Own Company?

No doubt, downturns in the economy, prolonged Bearish Phases, and the dreaded *R* word—*recession*—are scary times. However, some of the biggest companies began during the Great Depression and during cyclical downturns.

Even if you aren't as ambitious as, say, Thomas Edison, who started General Electric in 1890 during a global recession, there are allegedly "recession-proof" businesses to consider. Although not literally recession proof, several types of businesses (for example, health care, education, and law enforcement) are always in demand.

Candy consumption tends to rise during hard times. Cosmetic and nail-care businesses also tend to do well. Contraception sales go up. Luxury retailers excel. Alcohol and cigarette consumption increases. Even information technology (IT), particularly in software design and development, network and systems administration, and software implementation, has seen growth in bad cycles.

On the nastier side of life, repo businesses thrive, as do bankruptcy lawyers. The funeral business has a steady stream of clients during good and bad times. And what about tattoo parlors? I can barely think of one person under the age of thirty-five who does not have a tattoo somewhere. Moreover, that's just on the visible parts of their bodies. Statistically, "more than a third of Americans ages 18 to 25 have a tattoo, as well as 40 percent of folks in the 26 to 40 range. In contrast, studies found only about 10 percent of people age 41 to 64 are tattooed."[5]

Hey, Boomers—it is time for that tattoo!

The United States has had its share of recessions and Bear Phases. Interestingly, more than half of the Fortune 500 companies listed started up during a recession or bear market. Companies like Burger King, which began after the Korean War in 1953 during a tough economy, knew that, regardless, people must eat. Federal Express began operations in 1973; during the oil shock of 1973, a Yale student named Frederick Smith believed a company that could make fast deliveries to cities of all sizes was valuable.

Microsoft was kicked off in 1975. It was a time of rising unemployment, crazy out-of-control gas prices, and a sluggish GDP. CNN went on the air in 1980 at a time when the country was hearing "double-dip recession." We started MarketGauge.com during the dot-com bubble. Here we are, twenty years later, still going strong!

Guiding Your Children's College and Career Choices

Although stock prices and perhaps revenues shrink during a Bear Phase, that does not mean there aren't opportunities for career paths. I would not allow a defeatist attitude to prevent me from seeking a job or sending my kid off to college to pursue a major in an area in which he or she is interested. For example, my first career in special education—public school teachers and especially special education teachers are always in high demand! The Bureau of Labor Statistics (BLS) projects a 17 percent growth in demand for kindergarten and elementary school teachers from 2010 to 2020.

The Healthcare and Social Assistance sector has the highest projected job growth of any industry. They expect to add more than

5.7 million jobs by 2020. Particularly registered nurses, but also other areas of nursing, are in super-high demand. Because of the aging Baby Boomer population, demand for health care and home health aides is expected to rise by 70 percent. The military, pharmaceutical companies, veterinary services, and religious organizations are also places to look for career opportunities when the market and the economy are suffering.

A Note to Millennials

Now that this generation has cornered the largest portion of the workforce, many news stories have appeared about their mercurial nature. In the United States alone, some 64 percent expect to leave the company they are working for over the next five years. This has had an impact on many job sectors. It can also provide opportunities for those who prefer job security or a place to begin a new career.

Information technology is a perfect example. There's an overall lack of qualified IT workers, which has put these jobs in very high demand. As older workers retire, there aren't enough younger workers taking their place. Furthermore, the number of U.S. college students graduating with a computer science degree has declined dramatically since 2005 to its lowest level since 1986. That trend has led some analysts to predict a 15 percent decrease in the supply of IT workers between 2008 and 2038; analysts predict a 15 percent decrease in the supply of workers, while the need for experienced workers will increase by 25 percent.

So Millennials, considering that there are plenty of jobs out there for you and your highly educated friends, ponder whether you're doing yourselves a disservice by ignoring the opportunities in these high-growth industries. After all, as many of you wish to buy a home but cannot afford the down payment, the statistics show that it will take you nearly twenty-eight years to save enough money to buy a house.

Companies are trying hard to attract the younger generation. Perks such as student loan repayment, money for a wedding, extended parental leave, and luxury car leases are in vogue during the good times. Ultimately, job security takes center stage when times turn sour!

Summary

1. A true bear market is not a correction. We must remember that widespread pessimism and negative sentiment in a bear market can last for many months to a couple of years or even worse. Think of what happened in Japan.

2. There really is no hard-and-fast rule for how interest rates, the dollar, and the stock market all correlate with one another. During market crashes, it is generally a good idea to run into safety with cash. However, it is equally empowering to know whether your dollars will buy you more or less.

3. Lower oil and gas prices have some real benefits and some real consequences.

4. If by the time a Bear Phase is in the works you are already out of many risky stocks and into cash, bonds, or other asset classes that are outperforming, you are in great shape. This is the time to sit and wait for the Bear Phase to taper off.

5. Knowing which sector of the economy the company you work for is in would be helpful information. Check your company's chart if it is a publicly traded one. Once you see a chart of your industry or company go into a Caution Phase, you have time to take some steps to protect yourself before things move from bad to worse.

6. If you own a company, long before the economy goes into a tailspin, seeing the phase turn down into Cau-

tion is your signal to start protecting your business from financial ruin or bankruptcy!

7. Although stock prices and perhaps revenues shrink during a Bear Phase, that does not mean there aren't opportunities for career paths and for making investment decisions.

8. A Bear Phase eventually ends. Take advantage of reading phases to stay well ahead of the curve.

CHAPTER FOURTEEN

THE RECUPERATION PHASE—HOPE

I can say wholeheartedly that Recuperation is, hands down, my favorite phase. Hope returns. Those investors who were short or banking that the instrument or the overall market would fall begin to buy back or cover those positions. As selling pressure dries up, investors look to buy.

How Do I Identify a Recuperation Phase?

1. The 50-WMA (dotted line) is below the 200-WMA (solid line).

2. The slope on the 50-WMA should begin to neutralize or start to turn positive while the 200-WMA slope remains negative. That will take longer to stop its decline.

3. The price should be above the 50-WMA yet below the 200-WMA. The closer the price is to the 50-WMA, the lower the risk should the phase fail.

The S&P 500 chart in figure 14.1 is the quintessential example of a time when the public's nerves were still rattled, but the charts

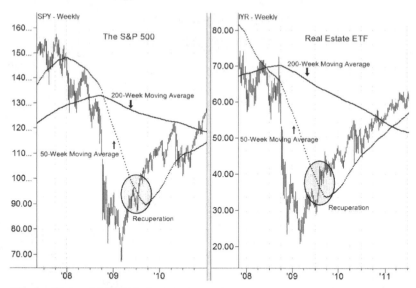

Figure 14.1. S&P 500 Cycle through Phases 2008–2010/Real Estate (IYR) Cycle through Phases 2008–2013 (Courtesy of TradeStation Technologies, Inc.)

relayed that the bottom was near. In July 2009, the price of SPY returned to above the 50-WMA. However, even though the Recuperation Phase gained momentum, it wasn't until the beginning of October 2009 that the slope on the 50-WMA turned positive. In July, the price sat very close to the 50-WMA but with a negative slope. Therefore, the probability of the phase holding was not optimal.

By October, when the slope began to turn upward, the price was a bit high relative to the 50-WMA. For investors, that increased the risk to below the 50-WMA. What was the best thing to do? Wait. In the spring of 2010, the price fell back to the 50-WMA, and the slope was still positive. Although the price fluctuated up and down the 50-WMA with a positive slope, my confidence in calling a bottom of the market grew.

For trading, by September 2010, SPY set up perfectly with the lowest amount of risk. Nevertheless, a year before that in October

2009, the public who watched phases could feel more confident that the worst was over, unless they watched the news.

Top Headlines 2009–2010

1. January 20, 2009: President Barack Obama takes the oath of office as the nation's forty-fourth president.

2. February 28, 2009: More than 650,000 Americans lose jobs for a record third straight month, bringing un-employment—now 12.5 million people—to a quarter-century peak of 8.1 percent nationally. Then, on September 30, the nation's jobless rate hits 9 percent, the highest in twenty-six years.

3. Despite a $787 billion federal stimulus package, much of the U.S. economy continues to sputter throughout the year. Scores of banks fail, the federal deficit triples to a record $1.4 trillion, and stocks fall to their lowest levels since 1997 before rallying. Yet investment banks' profits surge, triggering public anger.

4. Economy Struggles: Climbing out of the deepest recession since the 1930s, the economy grows at a healthy rate in the January–March quarter. Still, the gain comes mainly from companies refilling stockpiles they had let shrink during the recession. The economy can't sustain the pace. The lingering effects of the recession slow growth. The benefits of an $814 billion government stimulus program fade. Consumers cut spending in favor of building savings and slashing debt.

5. Real Estate Crisis: Housing remains depressed despite super-low mortgage rates. The average rate on a thirty-year fixed mortgage dips to 4.17 percent in November, the lowest in decades. In spite of this, home sales and

prices sink further. Nearly one in four homeowners owe more on their mortgages than their homes are worth, making it all but impossible for them to sell their house and buy another. An estimated one million families lose their homes to foreclosure.

6. European Bailouts: Greece and Ireland require emergency bailouts, raising fears that debt problems will spread and destabilize global markets. European governments and the International Monetary Fund agree to a $145 billion rescue of Greece in May and a $90 billion bailout of Ireland in November. The bailouts require both countries to slash spending, triggering protests by workers. Investors fear that debt troubles will spread to Spain, Portugal, and other countries, weaken the European Union, and threaten the future of the euro as its common currency.

The Headlines versus the Phases

One cannot minimize the impact of the 2008 mortgage and loan debacle on homeowners. Clearly, if you were one of the homeowners underwater, owing more on your house than it was worth, the IYR chart in figure 14.1 might be more of a frustration than a comfort. If that describes you, I also encourage you to look at the chart in a positive fashion and in the spirit meant. As the phases turn, hope springs eternal. As horrific as the events of 2008–2010 were financially, the Recuperation Phase is an accurate and hopeful sign that the worst in that sector was over.

However, in spite of the phase flipping into Recuperation Phase as of July 2009, there was nary a person who felt better. In fact, headlines such as "The Economy Can't Sustain the Pace" or "The Benefits of an $814 Billion Government Stimulus Program Fade" scared most people. Only those who watch phases could see that the Real Estate chart, for example, reflected a different tone. I showed you this chart specifically because the 2008 crash happened on the back of the real estate crisis; yet it was that very sector that held its ground above the 50-WMA, helping the rest of the market gain confidence.

I can promise you, though, that relatively few investors understood the importance of ignoring the news and focusing on the charts. Certainly, posttraumatic stress kept many financial planners away from investing. As you can see from the headline "Consumers Cut Spending in Favor of Building Savings and Slashing Debt," in the end, saving rather than investing was not the best idea. By early 2013, the price of the Real Estate ETF rose from thirty-five dollars to nearly seventy-five dollars.

The peak price in IYR occurred in the early part of 2015 at more than eighty-four dollars. Even if you waited to sell the ETF for a profit once it went into a Caution Phase in mid-2015, you still locked in more than 100 percent gains in that ETF alone. Furthermore, had you waited to liquidate when the 200-WMA broke in early 2016, you still made just under 100 percent gains.

A Classic (and Highly Profitable) Recuperation Phase

To begin with, try very hard not to listen to analysts who predict where the price of gold is heading. For example, back in 2011, certain analysts believed they were conservative in lowering their projection for a peak price in gold from $2,500 an ounce to $2,100. They got two things right: gold did go higher in 2011, and it peaked in price, but not at $2,100. The peak price was $1,917.90, reached in August 2011.

I remember that summer well. My dear friend's financial planner, whom she had been with for years, put her in the ETF for gold (GLD) at $170, or $1,700 per ounce, and told her not to worry since gold would hit $2,700 an ounce very soon. I wondered what took this person so long to buy gold. After all, the ETF GLD had entered a Bullish Phase in 2009, making him two and a half years too late.

In the beginning of 2009, when that phase improved to Bullish, the price of GLD was $87, or about $870 an ounce. I called my friend and suggested that she ask her financial planner where he thought he was wrong. How much was he willing to risk?

He answered that there was no risk. Seriously? No risk? After I calmed down from my near hysteria, I told my friend to get out of the gold market. I felt the gold move was over and about to fall dramatically. How did I know? I didn't really. At that point, it was more of a sense after years of trading experience. I have learned that when a position becomes saturated, the public is typically too late. You can almost bet they are buying at the top. In the spring of 2012, gold went into a brief Caution Phase. Caution, or merely a heads-up, should be taken as a sign that, most likely, the warning should not go ignored.

Then the price of the ETF rose back over the 50-WMA and back to a Bullish Phase. However, the slope on the 50-WMA began to decline. I called my friend again at the beginning of 2013 after I wrote a daily piece about how gold had topped out. At that point, she had the chance to get out and, with luck, break even. Her broker strongly advised against selling. In fact, he refused to sell.

I was once again aghast at this broker's behavior. GLD broke the 50-WMA hard, and the slope declined further and further. My friend finally got out of the trade by insisting that her broker sell her position for a nominal loss, though she had to threaten to pull her account from him.

I rarely intervene or interfere so emphatically with my friends' and associates' personal finances, as it is bad policy if you want to keep those friends and associates. In this case, I made an exception. Had my friend waited, as most of the public did, she would have lost a lot of money.

The death cross occurred in August 2013, two years from the peak. In the summer of 2013, gold "experts" predicted higher prices regardless of whether the Federal Reserve continued quantitative easing. The reality of the situation was that gold plummeted to nearly $1,000 an ounce at the end of 2015.

Gold 2015–2016

Figure 14.2 shows that the price of gold (GLD) took two different stabs above the 50-WMA. At the very beginning of 2015, it closed above the 50-WMA for two weeks in a row before selling off again. As slope reliably keeps us from chasing false phase-change signals, with the negative slope, we did not bite. Good thing, too, since GLD proceeded to reach a new low.

Then, at the end of 2015, the price peeked its head above the 50-WMA but did not close the week above that level. No signal. Fast-forward to January 2016; before the price pierced the 50-WMA, I noticed that the slope on the overhead 50-WMA turned neutral. Then, during the second week of February, GLD made a run for it. Not only did GLD close above the 50-WMA, but the slope also turned positive, transitioning into a picture-perfect Recuperation Phase. However, the same could not be said for the headlines:

> January 21, 2016: "Peak Gold and Silver May Have Come and Gone" ("There is good reason to believe that newly mined supplies of gold and silver will decline in 2016 and beyond").[1]

Figure 14.2. Gold Peak Bottom 2011–2016 (Courtesy of TradeStation Technologies, Inc.)

However, maybe you saw this:

February 11, 2016: "Gold Surges to 1-Year High on Financial Uncertainty" ("Investors are returning to gold as a core diversifier and safe haven investment").[2]

James Butterfill, head of research at ETF Securities, said in a note, "Given the increasingly challenging investment and economic environment, we expect this trend to continue."[3]

Regardless of whether you saw negative or positive predictions for the next move in GLD, the chart told the whole story. Why do I love the Recuperation Phase the most of all the phases? On the path to Oz, it truly keeps you on the Yellow Brick Road!

Remember Wal-Mart?

In chapter 9, "How to Avoid the Thorns," we looked at a weekly chart for Wal-Mart (WMT). In early 2015, WMT went from Bullish to Caution to Distribution and ended the year in a Bearish Phase. Besides illustrating a complete turn of the phase wheel, the chart also gave you a way to manage an investment for a stock like Wal-Mart. Since most publicly traded companies will do whatever they can to prop up their company's stock, WMT highlights that cycle to a tee.

By March 2016, Wal-Mart's price began to recover from the lows it posted in late 2015. WMT cleared the 50-WMA; yet the slope remained negative. By the beginning of 2017, WMT cleared both the 50- and the 200-WMA. Plus, the slope on those MAs turned positive. For phase watchers and investors, WMT gave several low-risk opportunities until the peak price posted in February 2018 at $109.98. Then, in mid-2018, it went back into a Caution Phase.

What Have You Learned Thus Far?

If you looked at the chart in figure 14.3 of the U.S. Oil Fund (USO) and thought that it could be about to turn from a Bearish Phase into a Recuperation Phase, then bravo! Furthermore, if you wanted to make your first investment or add to an existing portfolio by buying USO and thought that it must clear the 50-WMA first, bravo again!

Next, if you thought that you must see the slope on the 50-WMA neutralize and then point up, once more bravo! Finally, if you thought that the risk (or amount of money you are willing to lose) when and if USO clears the 50-WMA is relatively minimal based on its recent trading levels (support every time since April 2016 the price dropped to around ten dollars), then BRAVO!

Naturally, if you also thought that if oil goes up, that means more expensive gas for your car and heat for your home, then maybe not so fast on the bravo. However, if you make the investment by buying the ETF, you can more than make up for the increased costs. If you choose not to make the investment, at least you know well in advance and can take the necessary precautions. Just as the Caution Phase is our best advanced-warning system to make changes in our lives, investments, careers, and educational paths, the Recuperation Phase is the best time to start thinking about how to capitalize on the better times to come!

Figure 14.3. U.S. Oil Fund about to Improve Phase 2016 (Courtesy of TradeStation Technologies, Inc.)

Summary

1. The Recuperation Phase (my favorite one) is when the simple 50-WMA is below the 200-WMA. The price of the instrument trades above the 50-WMA after having been below that level for a considerable amount of time.

2. The slope on the 50-WMA should be neutral or just beginning to point up. The slope on the overhead 200-WMA slope remains negative. It will take longer to stop its decline.

3. There could very well be a disconnect between the head-lines that relay fear and the improved phase conditions in a stock, ETF, or stock index. That's okay—trust the phase.

4. As in the example of the gold ETF GLD, the Recuperation Phase, especially after a prolonged period of weak prices, can make you a lot of money with very low risk. By the time the headlines change to reflect the better conditions, you are already booking great profits!

5. There is no need to guess that a phase change might happen. In the right circumstances, the price will clear the 50-WMA, and the slope will turn. When and if the price is near enough to the 50-WMA, you can make decisions both financially and for your life with a lot more confidence. For investors, if the price returns below the 50-WMA, you can exit quickly for a minimal loss. This is true for all phase changes that fail to follow through.

CHAPTER FIFTEEN
MY FAVORITE PHASE

I n reality, nobody can ever be 100 percent certain about anything except "death and taxes."[1]

However, because of human weakness, people hope. Hope helps us to move on. Hope is our way of expecting the future to turn out better than the past. "In fact, a growing body of scientific evidence points to the conclusion that optimism (or hope) may be hardwired by evolution into the human brain."[2]

If hope is our natural inclination, then the natural progression after tough economic times into a Recuperation Phase not only makes perfect sense but also reinforces the cycle of human nature and the cycle of phases. Imagine, then, when hope snowballs into a collective consciousness, how that might affect the stock market and the economy.

According to Mark Ragins, MD, a leading psychiatrist in the recovery movement, recovery has four stages: "1. Hope 2. Empowerment 3. Self-Responsibility 4. A Meaningful Role in Life."[3]

In making stock investment decisions and for creating better opportunities in life, the *empowerment* of the Recuperation Phase begins with the ability to identify that phase. Subsequently, we must learn how to use it. Empowerment comes from having access to information and the opportunity to make our own choices. We can then focus on making gains instead of suffering losses.

From empowerment comes self-responsibility. Once you can solve your own problems, you open up doors. Once doors are open, your state of mind shifts from a scarcity mentality to one of abundance. You feel safer taking risks, trying new things, and learning from mistakes. Once we take a risk and succeed, we create a new paradigm.

Experts will tell you that economic recoveries are recognizable several months after they begin. Economists use data such as unemployment numbers to analyze the state of the economy. That helps them determine whether a recovery is indeed in progress.

We do not have to rely on the experts or the economists. We have a reliable system with phases using the Weekly Moving Averages. Once we see that a Recuperation Phase is taking place in any particular sector of the economy, stock market index, or individual company or raw material, we can take immediate action. And we can do so with minimal risk.

Figure 15.1 shows a four-chart screen of Real Estate (IYR), Biotechnology (IBB), the Russell 2000 (IWM), and Semiconductors (SMH) ETFs. Biotech and Semiconductors are the two sectors that best represent how invested speculators are in the overall market. Real Estate, another reliable measure of how the U.S. economy has been doing since the crash of 2008, began to recover at the same time.

At the start of 2009, all four ETFs priced under the 50- and 200-WMAs, indicating they were in Bearish Phases. The first sector that caught my eye back in the spring of 2009 was Biotechnology because the position of the Moving Averages was curious. Notice that the 50-WMA crossed beneath the 200-WMA much later than the other three ETFs. Therefore, I could see it entered a Bearish Phase almost after the fact since the others did so in 2008. It dawned on me that the sector that captures the most speculative money was the last to go negative. Typically, the money that is last to get in on major up or down trends is a reliable signal that it is too late.

Figure 15.1. Signs of Recovery Real Estate, Biotechnology, Semiconductors, Russell 2000 2009–2010 (Courtesy of TradeStation Technologies, Inc.)

By late June and early July 2009, Biotechnology again cleared the 50-WMA into a Recuperation Phase. So did the Russell 2000, Semiconductors, and finally, by mid-July, Real Estate. With speculative money coming back into the Biotech sector and with the other three major areas of the U.S. economy also coming back, the opportunity to take advantage of the bottom and the new Recuperation Phases presented itself to those in the know.

From hope and empowerment comes self-responsibility. By the fall of 2009, the slopes on the 50-WMAs all turned positive. Biotechnology took the lead, crossing back over the 200-WMA before the others did. I did not need an economist or a market analyst to tell me that the worst was over. I could see the phase changes and the leadership in a sector where some "smart" money was last to get out also indicated that a lot of the "smart" money was the first to get back in.

I Make Less Than $30,000 a Year; What Can I Do?

A staggering 40 percent of the U.S. population has an overall negative net worth. In the United States, wealth inequality or the "unequal distribution of assets," remains prevalent. In the spirit of writing a fully inclusive guide, I thought long and hard about how to make this book relevant for those who most likely owe more money than they have.

A negative net worth does not automatically mean you live in poverty. Paying off a mortgage and student and car loans can put you in that category. The poorest Americans who have jobs are barely able to count on rising wages to help pull them out of debt. Furthermore, statistically, the wealth and income divide deepens across racial and ethnic lines. Naturally, it's easier to save money when there is income growth. However, currently, the poorest spend far more than they earn.

Nearly half of Americans would not be able to come up with $400 in savings in an emergency, according to a Federal Reserve study. America's poor and its middle class live on the razor's edge of financial security throughout their working years and are often ill prepared for retirement. The United States finished nineteenth for three consecutive years in a global analysis of retirement security, behind Australia, New Zealand, Japan, South Korea, Canada, and thirteen European countries.[4]

Between flat wages and increased expenditures, many households find it very difficult (if not impossible) to save any money. However, another interesting statistic highlights that "millions of lower-income people can collectively devote tens of billions of dollars to an investment vehicle that holds the promise of future wealth."[5]

A perfect example of this concept is lottery tickets.

The lottery is a $70 billion government-financing initiative disproportionately funded by the poor—an indication that low-income people see lotteries as a kind of savings vehicle. Rather than put $200 per year away in a low-risk, low-reward savings account, some put $200 into high-risk, high-reward lottery tickets.[6]

If you buy lottery tickets or spend money on things you can temporarily live without (the extra TV, cell phone, etc.), you fall into this category, and there just might be room to save little bits of money at a time. If so, to help get your investing feet wet, there are ways to invest small amounts of money at a time to try to make that money grow. Whether you invest large or small amounts of money, the principle of phases doesn't change.

I chose to address those with an income of $30,000 or less in the Recuperation Phase chapter because it allows one to buy when prices are very low. It also offers the lowest amount of risk if you can time your way into a trade when the price is closest to the 50-WMA. Even with a small amount of money (ignoring the hyperbolic promises of how you will "get rich quick" and turn $1,000 into $1,000,000 in just a few months), it is possible to make your money grow in a much safer fashion. Once you grow your account and gain experience, you can increase the investment over time.

Mini Trading Accounts

Most standard trading accounts using a trading platform such as TradeStation require a minimum balance of $5,000 to start. Certain companies allow you to open up a mini account. Mini accounts are ideal for investors who are new to the market. Some allow a minimum investment of $250.

Companies such as Vanguard require a minimum investment of $1,000. TD Ameritrade does not require a minimum investment amount but does require a $2,000 deposit. Robinhood Markets requires no minimum deposit and no trading fees for U.S.-listed stocks or ETFs. All instruments follow the same rules for phase changes. All that matters is that you can identify the phase and see whether the phase looks strong or weak by assessing the slope of the Moving Averages. Then you can determine how far the price is from the Moving Averages so you can figure out how much risk you are taking should the phase fail. Foreign exchange (FOREX) is an institution or system for dealing in the currency of other countries.

Before you commit any money, do an internet search of the investment company and read customer reviews. You will also need to find out whether the company charges commissions, if there are initial fees, and (if so) how much.

Using the Recuperation Phase to Make Smart Investment Choices

Low Interest Rates and Low Housing Prices

A substantial reason the market began its recovery is attributable to the Federal Reserve flooding the market with dollars that bought up bonds. Interest rates fell dramatically. Although quantitative easing stopped in late 2014, interest rates have gotten lower and lower. What makes this phenomenon of low rates during a market recovery so tantalizing is the opportunity to borrow money cheaply.

Perhaps one of the greatest investment options for both buying the ETF as a trade and looking at real estate purchases was the intersection of the housing market in recovery while the interest rates began to fall. After the crash in 2008, real estate prices slowly began to recover from the lows.

As of late 2009, IYR had already climbed back into a Recuperation Phase. The Long Bonds (and note the reverse relationship: as TLT price rises, the interest rate drops) waffled around the Moving Averages throughout 2010–2011. By mid-2011, the TLTs exploded, and rates plummeted until the summer of 2016. That meant you could shop for a house at much lower prices than was possible just a few years earlier at the housing peak and get a super-low-rate mortgage as well.

Indeed, loans have been harder to secure given tighter restrictions for applicants to meet credit requirements. Nevertheless, for those who could secure approval, the opportunity was historic.

If you were already a homeowner and could afford to do so, buying an investment property and then mortgaging it at a thirty-year rate of 3 percent was a golden opportunity. You could easily rent out the home, not only covering the mortgage payment but also providing positive cash flow for yourself each month.

If you were a renter unable to qualify for loan approval for a traditional mortgage on your own or make a 20 percent down payment, you could potentially enter a real estate contract with your landlord. This would allow you to make rental payments toward a purchase price with an eventual agreement to own the home. The rate may not be as advantageous as a bank would provide, but it would still lock you in near the mortgage rate lows. In addition, you would have all of the benefits of owning your own home. Of course, refinancing an existing home that has enough equity in it has been a good idea that has gotten better since 2009.

The trend of low mortgage rates continued from 2014 until September 2016. With the anticipation of the Federal Reserve raising rates by the end of 2016 and into 2017, the TLTs dropped, as yields went higher. Meanwhile, the Real Estate ETF went from a Recuperation Phase into a Bullish Phase. The brief dip in early 2016 in the ETF turned out to be a new, low-priced buy opportunity. As of this writing, the Real Estate ETF had sold off from the highest price, yet continued to hold a price level above the 200-WMA. This makes sense given the sudden move lower in TLTs. Once TLTs went into a Caution Phase, refinancing made sense, as it signaled interest rates would begin to rise.

Housing prices have gone up around most of the United States since 2008 (though it is always best to check individual cities and towns). The relatively low interest rates still make refinancing advantageous because there is a good chance your home has appreciated, or gone up in value. Given the charts in figure 15.1, it could also mean the historic rates have reversed the trend and could work their way higher.

The Russell 2000's Alter Ego and Stepbrother Utilities

For our purposes, we can call the ETF for the Utilities sector of the economy "Uncle" or XLU. The *Merriam-Webster's Dictionary* definition of *utility* is "the quality or state of being useful, a service (such as a supply of electricity or water) that is provided to the public."

The Utilities sector is a high-yielding equity investment that pays dividends. Dividends are sums of money typically paid quarterly by a company to its shareholders out of the company's profits. It is sensitive to changes in interest rates. A higher interest rate means that the cost of capital is higher. Conversely, lower interest rates make Utilities more attractive. With the environment of lower interest rates, the overall sector has done extremely well since 2009. Similar to the unique opportunity Real Estate offered because of the low interest rates, Utilities have yielded investors huge profits. Furthermore, for those who are looking for an area of growth to explore career or educational possibilities, this sector provides a myriad of prospects.

XLU, the Utilities ETF

In 2010, XLU entered a strong Recuperation Phase with a rising slope on the 50-WMA. By the end of 2011, it went into a Bullish Phase. Since then, XLU tested the Bullish Phase by entering into a Caution Phase several times throughout 2013–2014.

In 2015, after an initial surge in price, XLU went back into and stayed in a Caution Phase until early 2016. At the halfway point of 2016, XLU made new all-time highs.

Economists and analysts have studied the relationship between stocks and Utilities. The relationship may help predict future trends in both. The conventional wisdom is that "during periods of economic fragility and volatility in financial markets, the Utilities sector tends to outperform broader cyclical trades."[7]

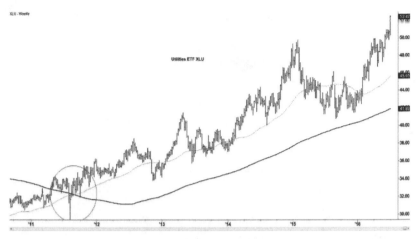

Figure 15.2. Utilities from Caution to Bullish 2012–2016 (Courtesy of TradeStation Technologies, Inc.)

Their research indicates that the relationship between stocks and the small caps or Russell 2000 and Utilities can "serve as a warning sign of increased volatility and extreme market movement in the short-term."[8]

During the periods when XLU improves over stocks, it serves as fair warning to keep eyes on the next move in the Russell 2000.

For our purposes, these sudden and more volatile changes in price between Utilities and the Russell 2000 are more relevant if the weekly phase changes on either or both as well. With XLU trading at new all-time highs by November 2017, the Russell 2000 was still a considerable distance away from its all-time high.

For the more sophisticated trader, if the Russell 2000 cannot catch up to XLU or if IWM fails to hold up in price, that could be a sign something more volatile and perhaps nastier is forthcoming. However, I urge even sophisticated traders to follow the phase changes and not necessarily anticipate that historical relationships will work or, if they do, work for very long. As an aside, another possible scenario, since Utilities are extremely interest-rate sensitive, is that the outperformance of Utilities over the small caps will be a harbinger of some change in interest-rate policy on the horizon. The reverse is true as well. If Utilities underperform, that could predict higher rates on the horizon.

The Recuperation Phase in Utilities Presents Education and Career Opportunities

Besides the dividends investors receive, another reason that some utility companies such as Exelon (EXC) have done so well more recently and represent an even more roseate future is the changing landscape to clean energy.

To confirm a growing trend, Bloomberg New Energy Finance published a report in 2015 that showed a record amount of money invested into renewable energy. With a steady rise in renewables in both China and Europe coupled with diminishing costs to convert to wind and solar energy, many view renewables as a permanent game changer worldwide.

In the world of Utilities, electricity-industry leaders already agree that the switch to renewable energy sources will dominate their grid systems. California's grid system already gets 30 percent of its electricity from renewable energy. On certain days, that number can climb to 50 percent.

Other states such as New York, Vermont, and Hawaii have plans to convert large percentages of their electricity to renewables as well. New York hopes to be at 50 percent by 2050, Vermont at 90 percent by 2050, and Hawaii at 100 percent by 2045. This means that, regardless of what the stock market does, if Utilities outperform stocks, the future in utility companies could be solid.

The ETF XLU, like all ETFs, comprises a basket of different company stocks. At the time of writing, NextEra Energy, Inc. (NEE), had 9.13 percent and held the largest weight in XLU's ETF basket. Researching any ETF company's holdings is as easy as logging on to the internet and looking up the ETF symbol.

NextEra Energy went into a Recuperation Phase at the end of 2010. The Bullish or golden cross occurred in late 2011. As many folks were still trying to recover from the 2008 crash in housing and the overall economy, phase watchers could see the comeback happening in Utilities. NEE is just one good example.

Furthermore, if, as an investor, you felt better and safer buying Utilities stocks or certain companies in that sector in 2010, the opportunity presented itself with extremely low risk. Since the Federal Reserve made no secret of its intention to keep interest rates low, that only provided a better scenario for investors in XLU or the individual companies in that ETF.

For trading, I like to use the technical analysis of the weekly chart and the corresponding phases to guide me for longer-term trends. The daily charts also have phases and are reliable indicators for the more active investors. In the world of trading, one can focus on many time frames. It's all a matter of style.

Concerning fundamental analysis, I make no claims that I research quarterly results in price and earnings ratios or estimated earnings per share. A fundamental analysis is a method of analyzing a security to determine its underlying economic values using financial statements that incorporate assets, liabilities, and earnings. When any company I am interested in reports its quarterly earnings, I take note. However, I focus mainly on the companies whose charts and phases are set up for a low risk, well before an earnings report is available.

However, I do use a different level of fundamental analysis. My way of defining the fundamentals is how the company, commodity, or currency may be shaped by a megatrend either in its infancy or as it matures. Hence, the Utilities sector and the gradual shift to renewable energy interests me.

You can track a megatrend in its infancy and then find a corresponding sector entering a Recuperation Phase. From there, you can pare the sector down to individual companies to see how each fits into the megatrend and the phase. The NextEra Energy website looks like most other company websites. For a description of the company, use the tabs at the top of your computer screen to access "Our Company" or a similarly named option.

Here's what NextEra has to say: "NextEra Energy is focused on building long-term value for our shareholders by investing in energy technologies that are designed to provide affordable, clean and reliable power for our customers. In 2014, we generated more electricity from the wind and sun than any other company in the world."

Now you know you are looking at a good company in the Utilities sector that is working toward renewables. Another tab typically takes you to "Investor Relations," the place to find news affecting the company and events such as conference calls and earnings dates. There, should you be so inclined, you can download annual reports, Security and Exchange Commission filings, stock information, and corporate governance.

The tab for "Careers" contains vital information. For NextEra Energy, I learned there are 15,000 employees located in twenty-six states, Canada, and Spain. The company offers many types of job opportunities, including engineering, nuclear energy, information technology, and business analysis. They tout an inclusive environment with particular emphasis on hiring those who served in the military.

On the bottom of the "Careers" page, there are links to "How to Apply" and their "Hiring Process." NextEra includes job titles and descriptions that you can specifically apply to online. I also read about their range of internship opportunities and the qualifications required. Regarding education requirements, the company offers monetary assistance toward tuition. They have their own university that has more than two hundred classrooms and online offerings that focus on leadership development, business/commercial skills, professional effectiveness, and quality improvement. NextEra breaks down the courses of study in their university into seven different colleges. Whether you are interested in human resources, nuclear power, or customer service and sales, they will help you reach your professional development goals and improve your competencies.

Almost all companies' websites in every field or sector have a plethora of information for you to look at. I remember the olden days of sending out résumés and hoping you mailed yours to the right person in the company. Then you hoped your résumé wasn't filed in the "circular file" (wastebasket). You had no way to track the jobs offered or find out whether they had training for that job. You had to wait for months before you received a rejection or acceptance notification. And that was only if the Human Resources Department was kind enough to follow up. Now, you have a way to track sectors and companies that are growing by using the weekly phases. Talk about a megatrend that keeps maturing, and you can do it all online!

Summary

1. As people have a tendency to hope, the natural progression after tough economic times is for the economy to start to improve. Going from a Bearish Phase into a Recuperation Phase not only makes perfect sense but also reinforces the cycle of human nature and the cycle of phases.

2. Watching the Russell 2000 and the other five key U.S. economic sectors is a reliable way to track the economy's cycles. By following phases, you are well ahead of the curve.

3. The Recuperation Phase is the optimum time to invest. Even if you make less than $30K a year, there are ways to save and invest small amounts of money.

4. The low-interest-rate environment since the first quantitative easing by the Federal Reserve has provided unique opportunities in many sectors of the economy. When the Real Estate sector entered a Recuperation Phase, it

offered homeowners the chance to buy investment prop-
erties or refinance existing homes, locking in historically
low interest rates.

5. The Utilities sector not only pays dividends to investors
but also can relay future economic trends by looking at
its relationship with overall stocks. For those people who
are college bound or seeking a new career, the Utilities
sector is the perfect example of how to use the phases to
make informed decisions.

CHAPTER SIXTEEN

ACCUMULATION PHASE—OPTIMISM

M y sophomore and junior years in high school occurred during the late 1960s. Although I excelled in school, by that point the restlessness of my generation distracted me. I made it through those years as an honor student because I was a proficient studier. However, most of the high school subjects one was required to take in order to graduate didn't hold a candle to the events that were happening outside the classroom, except for one course—*geometry*!

Long before I thought about stocks, commodities, and trading, I loved geometry. Line segments, rays, parallel and perpendicular lines, angles, and so on, made sense to me in a time when so many other happenings in the world did not. The idea that you can prove a formula such as the area of a triangle gave me a tremendous sense of security.

Turns out, the technical analysis or study of charts and phases has a significant basis in geometry! Trend lines are actually rays that begin at one point and extend forever (well, in trading nothing is forever) in one direction up or down. Parallel lines are what we use to draw channels. Sequences and patterns are the fundamental principles behind the Fibonacci sequence, named after the Italian mathematician Leonardo of Pisa, known as "Fibonacci." *Liber Abaci*,

PLANT YOUR MONEY TREE

his book published in 1202, introduced the sequence to European mathematics.

Most people I know cannot recite from memory geometric formulas they learned in high school or tell you how to write a proof. However, all of my friends, even those less fascinated by math, can tell you what the Pythagorean Theorem is.

That theorem has nothing to do with phases. But as I did my research on the Accumulation Phase and its position at eleven o'clock on the phase wheel, I fell upon the man responsible for that theorem: Pythagoras himself. Pythagoras, best known as a Greek mathematician, believed that "all is number." He thought that the entire universe is mathematically precise.

As numbers have symbolic meanings, Pythagoras said that every concept or idea, even the most abstract ones, were associated with a number. He opined that some "higher good" created the number one. He called the number one a monad and the true generator of all numbers. To Pythagoras, the number one was the number of reason. This made me wonder what two ones together, or the number eleven, might imply. The generator of all numbers doubled? Intriguing.

As I continued to dig around, I found out that in modern times, schools of thought have taken Pythagoras's beliefs one step further. I have a friend who fixates on 11:11. If he looks at his watch and it says 11:11, he shudders. Taking Pythagoras's notion of the number one and my friend's phobia about the number eleven, I became fascinated with seeing whether I could find a correlation between the phobia, the Accumulation Phase, and the collective consciousness of investors during that phase.

I have friends who believe that if they continually see the number 11 or 111, it is because the universe is sending them a message. What message? According to Doreen Virtue, author of a best-selling book[1] and student of Pythagorean numerology, "one who sees 11, 111, or 1111 should keep thoughts positive and focus on desires rather than fears." For my dear friend who tends to see 11:11 quite often, I have suggested that he shift his reaction from shuddering to excitement.

The Accumulation Phase at eleven o'clock on the phase wheel is the "public participation phase" according to the Dow Theory. Furthermore, it follows the Recuperation Phase, or the phase of hope. *Merriam-Webster's Dictionary* defines *accumulation* as follows: "The acquisition or gradual gathering of something. The accumulation of wealth. A mass or quantity of something that has gradually gathered or been acquired."

Therefore, if we combine Pythagoras, Ms. Virtue, the dictionary meaning, and the position of the Accumulation Phase on the phase wheel at eleven o'clock, it starts to make a lot of sense.

How Do I Identify an Accumulation Phase?

1. The 50-WMA (dotted line) is below the 200-WMA (solid line).

2. The slope on the 50-WMA is positive. The slope on the 200-WMA is beginning to neutralize after a long period of negative slope.

3. The price or cost of the financial instrument in dollars is now above both the 50- and the 200-WMA.

The Accumulation Phase comes after a Recuperation Phase. Demand for that particular instrument is increasing. Investors begin to accumulate positions because during an Accumulation Phase, smart money adds to the positions they bought during the Recuperation Phase.

Unlike the "smart" investors who buy or buy more during an Accumulation Phase, the public is largely out of stocks and other financial instruments. Naturally, now that you are a phase watcher, you may already be involved in investing during the Recuperation Phase along with the smart money. Once an instrument enters an

Accumulation Phase, traders that are more active could consider taking partial profits.

Watching the slope on the two major Weekly Moving Averages helps investors determine the strength or weakness of the Accumulation Phase. If the slope on the 200-WMA is pointing down once an instrument enters an Accumulation Phase, the likelihood of it failing is greater. If the slope on the 200-WMA is neutral or pointing up, then the Accumulation Phase will likely bring in even more buyers.

Figure 16.1 shows two examples of how the slope on the 200-WMA (solid line) helps you to determine whether the Accumulation Phase will strengthen or weaken. One example has not reached an Accumulation Phase yet. I put it there, though, so you can begin to think like an investor.

The first chart, Federal Express (FDX), dates back to 2010–2011. Notice that the slope on the 50-WMA points sharply higher. When FDX went into a Recuperation Phase, the move from sixty dollars a share to about eighty-five dollars was swift and painless.

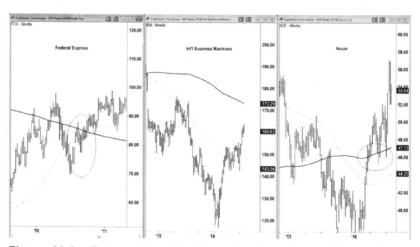

Figure 16.1. Determining the Strength of an Accumulation Phase: Federal Express, IBM, Nucor (Courtesy of TradeStation Technologies, Inc.)

Then, in March–April 2010, FDX continued the upward price move to clear the 200-WMA.

What do you see? The slope on the 200-WMA is still negative. Any surprise then that the buying euphoria abated, and the price dropped back down to seventy dollars per share by the beginning of June? The chart on the far right shows exactly the opposite. Nucor Corporation (NUE), the largest steel producer in the United States, entered a Recuperation Phase at the beginning of March 2016. Notice the slope on the overhead 200-WMA; it was neutral, and by the time the price rose above it, it was positive. The price fluctuated for a while around the 200-WMA, until the uptrend resumed in June.

This chart completely supports the notion that "smart money" had already begun to buy. The public, nonetheless, remained outside of steel. In fact, headlines told the public that the steel industry could not rally. When do you think the public began to buy NUE? July 2016. If you were a phase watcher and saw NUE go into a Recuperation Phase in the beginning of March when it cleared the then-neutral slope on the 50-WMA, you bought around forty-four dollars. The public bought at fifty-six dollars. You are making money and locking in profits. The public is sweating it out, having bought high.

The middle chart is there for educational purposes and for fun. In March 2016, IBM cleared the 50-WMA and entered a Recuperation Phase. What would you say about that phase? Strong? Weak? How is the slope on the 50-WMA? Up? Down? Neutral?

If you said "down," you're correct! However, in June 2016, the slope on the 50-WMA neutralized, and by the end of July, it had turned up. If you were interested in buying IBM, the chance came when the price dropped back down close to the 50-WMA while the slope turned positive, or at around $150 per share. Here's the fun part: What do you see on the overhead 200-WMA? How is the slope? What is the price that IBM needs to trade at in order for it to get into an Accumulation Phase? Do you think it will eventually trade up to that level? If it does, will it be a strong or weak phase?

Answers: The slope on the overhead 200-WMA is negative. The price it needs to clear for IBM to enter an Accumulation Phase is $173. Based on the strengthening of the Recuperation Phase, there is a good chance IBM will trade up to the 200-WMA. Unless the slope on the 200-WMA turns positive, those who bought at around $150 should consider taking partial profits.

Headlines 2010–2011 and the U.S. Economic Sectors

In 2010, an uneasy economy dominated the headlines. In March 2010, the Federal Reserve launched "quantitative easing 2," or QE2. They would purchase another $600 billion of longer-term Treasury securities over the course of several months.

However, with a growing financial crisis in Europe, fears over the stubbornly high unemployment rate, talk of a double-dip recession, and the historic health-care-reform law all creating anxiety, on May 5, 2010, the Dow fell from an April high of 11,000 down to 10,000 in a matter of sixteen minutes. By the end of May 5, the Dow recovered 653 points of that 1,000-point decline. Then again, on June 4, the Dow closed just under 10,000. The battle of the bears and the bulls dragged on.

For the economic sectors and phase watchers, decision making came a bit easier. The first sector to head into an Accumulation Phase was Biotechnology (IBB).

By the end of 2010, Biotechnology, already in a Bullish Phase, helped boost the confidence of the four other crucial economic sectors. Retail (XRT) and Semiconductors (SMH) were first to follow Biotech's lead, both taking an express train from Bearish to Recuperation to Accumulation to Bullish, all in a matter of roughly one and a half years.

Transportation (IYT) sprang to life in September 2010. The Russell 2000 (IWM) spent most of 2010 waffling between a Recuperation and an Accumulation Phase. Just as 2010 was ending, IWM cleared the 50- and 200-WMAs and then, with the golden cross, entered a Bullish Phase. The holdout, Regional Banks (KRE), proves the point of taking heed when divisiveness persists. Throughout 2010 and 2011, Regional Banks never cleared the 200-WMA. The weakness in that sector showed up as a stark contrast to the strength in the other four sectors that played out in the summer of 2011.

Headlines 2011–2012 and the Economic Sectors

The year 2011 began with optimism. The lead news stories in January of that year stated a renewed optimism in investing in stocks. Low interest rates had a lot to do with that optimism. An 11 percent rally in the Dow in 2010 helped as well. However, high unemployment rates continued. And, rearing its ugly head, a debate began on whether to raise the federal debt ceiling.

Simply put, the idea of a debt limit began in 1917 during World War I. The intention was to help Congress avoid having to approve every expenditure by the Treasury while at the same time allowing Congress to have control over those expenditures by imposing a spending limit. Back in 2010, the Treasury warned that the government would default if the United States did not meet its commitments to pay for obligations such as Social Security, Medicare, and the wars in Iraq and Afghanistan. Presently, the United States still has a substantial debt issue.

Many lawmakers did not want the debt ceiling increased and were willing to risk default because they believed it might force Congress to cut spending. By July 14, 2011, the major credit-rating agency, Standard and Poor's, placed the U.S. sovereign rating on "CreditWatch with negative implications." On August 5, 2011, Standard and Poor's downgraded the U.S. credit rating from AAA to AA+. Although the government was able to reach a bipartisan agreement, the credit-rating agency felt it was not enough to take care of the nation's debt for the long term.

We already determined that the Accumulation Phases in all of the key economic sectors besides Regional Banks were ephemeral. The rapid rise from Bearish to Accumulation to Bullish throughout most of 2011 proved investors had a growing appetite for stocks.

Then, with the debt-ceiling debate and the deterioration of the U.S. credit rating, none of "the family" remained immune to a massive drop in price. Although no longer in Accumulation Phases since the 50-WMA rose above the 200-WMA, interestingly, the family held the 200-WMA on the decline, all except Regional Banks. Furthermore, Retail, Biotechnology, Transportation, and the Russell 2000 quickly bounced up from the 200-WMA, thus reentering Bullish Phases by the start of 2012. Regional Banks (KRE) finally joined the rest after the beginning of 2012. Of the six, Regional Banks best represented the Accumulation Phase at that point.

Why Did Regional Banks Finally Catch Up?

First, remember that interest rates continued to decline. The Federal Reserve did yet another round of quantitative easing, or QE3. Had I written this book at any other point in history, I guarantee you that although interest rate policy has played a sizable role in the U.S. economy since the days of Paul Volcker, at no time has that policy been as critical to the overall picture as it has been since 2008.

Second, with European issues in the news, the big U.S. banks began to look more attractive to investors. Regional Banks has an even greater advantage in that the sector does not have the same level of exposure to sovereign debt crises. It is not regulated regarding trading activity as much as the big banks are.

By mid-2012, Regional Banks joined the rest of the family in a Bullish Phase. In 2013, everyone in the family enjoyed a massive run higher. Remember, if the members of the family are in alignment, you can invest more confidently. If the members are discordant, take that as fair warning to remain cautious.

Outside the Economic Sectors—the U.S. Federal Budget Spending and Phases

In 2012–2013, as part of budget cuts, the Fed cut defense spending from $900.7 billion to $777.7 billion. Although by 2015 it crept back up, the overall defense budget is less than what it was in 2011.

Many analysts predicted that the reduction in spending would lead to sharp declines in certain defense companies. Purposely avoiding any personal commentary on U.S. policies, I wish to show you how statistics, analyst projections, and phases do not always line up. My intention here, and throughout this book, is to help you make your own decisions based on what chart phases say. Dependency on the opinions of others and even fact-based analysis is great for cocktail party conversation; however, it will not necessarily help you make good financial or life decisions.

Considering the chart in figure 16.2, think about how much more you will impress your friends and acquaintances at a cocktail

Figure 16.2. Lockheed Martin 2011–2016 (Courtesy of TradeStation Technologies, Inc.)

party when you tell them that the charts of the defense stocks and the talk of a shrinking military budget do not add up!

Lockheed Martin (LMT) is a global security and aerospace company. Lockheed Martin and Martin Marietta merged in 1995. Their primary focus is defense, security, and advanced technologies. The LMT stock symbol lists in Aerospace/Defense Products and Services Industry and in the Industrial Goods sector.

According to the chart, in 2011 LMT fluctuated between Bearish and Recuperation Phases. Although the analysts were right about one thing—the defense budget would fall after 2011—they were completely wrong in thinking that defense-company stocks would fall in kind. In fact, just the opposite happened. LMT had just a short stay in the Accumulation Phase. With only a five-month period between January 2012 and May 2012 spent in an Accumulation Phase, LMT quickly rose into a Bullish Phase in the second half of 2012.

At the end of 2011, LMT went into a strong Recuperation Phase as the slope on the 50-WMA began to point upward. Smart money began buying then. In early 2012, you could have interpreted the Accumulation Phase as somewhat suspect because the slope on the 200-WMA continued to point downward. However, as autumn 2012 approached and into 2013, both the 50- and the 200-WMA slopes began to rise.

Since mid-2013, this stock has not looked back. Interpret the correlation between defense spending and Lockheed's performance any way you see fit. The bottom line is that phases empower you to make much more informed and timely decisions.

In Lockheed Martin, the transition from Bearish to Recuperation to Accumulation to Bullish happened relatively quickly. Savvy investors have made big money in this stock. Small investors did well, too. And if you still choose not to take advantage of investing in stocks, at the very least applying for a job in this or many other defense companies is a good idea!

Summary

1. The Accumulation Phase is when the 50-WMA sits below the 200-WMA. The price, or dollar amount, of that instrument works its way above both the 50- and the 200-WMA.

2. The slope on the 50-WMA may already be rising. The slope on the 200-WMA begins to flatten or the slope moves up.

3. The Accumulation Phase follows the Recuperation Phase. Hope turns into optimism. If the slope on the 200-WMA is pointing down, the likelihood of a failed Accumulation Phase is greater; if, however, the slope on the 200-WMA is neutral or pointing up, then the Accumulation Phase will strengthen and attract more buyers.

4. Accumulation Phases offer investors and folks seeking to make different or new life and career choices an opportunity to see discrepancies between headlines and charts. "Smart money" waits for both Recuperation and Accumulation Phases to enter the market before the public does.

5. The key U.S. economic sectors help you ascertain how the "real" U.S. economy is doing without relying on economists or market experts. Even if headlines read *disaster*, unified economic sectors all entering Accumulation Phases at the same time suggests that the market is ahead of the curve. By the time the public and headlines catch up, you are already booking big profits.

CHAPTER SEVENTEEN
FOLLOWING THE SMART MONEY

I f the Recuperation Phase got you to think about investing in stocks, buying a house, changing careers, or planning your kids' education, the Accumulation Phase is your confirmation. If you missed the Recuperation Phase because you didn't believe the bad times were really over, or you were still struggling to switch gears from scarcity to abundance, then the Accumulation Phase gives you another chance.

Note that even with the improvement in phases from Bearish to Recuperation to Accumulation, market sentiment typically remains negative. That means if you are looking to make an investment while the media continue to preach doom and gloom, you are most likely buying when many other retail investors have thrown in the towel with no intention of jumping back in.

Typically, the Accumulation Phase requires patience. An Accumulation Phase can fail, especially if the slope on the 200-week Moving Average is negative. So for the smaller investor, patience is required to wait for the slope to neutralize.

Although "smart money" often buys during the Recuperation Phase and then adds to the buying during the Accumulation Phase, oftentimes they do so with a willingness to wait years, if necessary, for the price to increase.

Most of us, however, do not have either the patience or the deep pockets. We want instant gratification. That is why I love the Recuperation Phase and often find the Accumulation Phase frustrating. As I get older, I am trying to master patience.

I hate losing money during the Accumulation Phase. More than any other phase, this phase tests my patience and my resolve on a trade, and for good reasons.

A Prime Example—Gold

I have purposely not covered a lot about risk in this book. The idea of how much risk is acceptable or where to place a stop (in layman's terms, the price at which you wish to exit the stock should the investment go against you) has many variables. I know traders who spend a lifetime mastering how big or small a position (or how many shares they should buy or sell) well in advance of actually making the investment. Professionals understand how position size relates to risk. The simplest way to ascertain your personal risk should you buy or sell when a phase changes is to figure out how much money you can afford to lose should the phase fail.

This brings me back to the point of why I chose to use phases on weekly rather than daily charts. Indeed, the six-phase analysis works for different time frames; yet, for longer-term investors and particularly for those making important decisions about real estate, careers, and education, weekly phase changes help you avoid market volatility. It considerably decreases the chance you will make some substantial change in your life only to regret it a short time thereafter. Nor do longer-term investors want to move money in and out of the market quickly. And you do not want to change careers only to find out you have moved into a fledgling industry.

Looking at the gold ETF chart GLD (figure 17.1), we can examine risk and longer-term investments. We can assess how people might fare if they are first considering a career that relates to buying and selling gold. At the end of 2015, I watched this chart carefully.

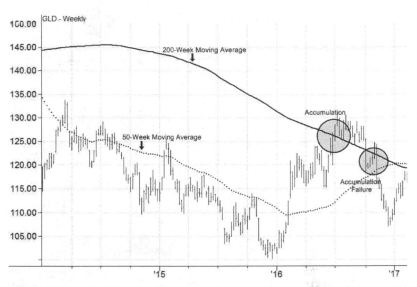

Figure 17.1. Gold from Recuperation to Accumulation 2014–2016/ Gold Fails Accumulation Phase—Slope Negative 2016 (Courtesy of TradeStation Technologies, Inc.)

Call it horse sense, but I had a feeling the bottom was close. However, I do practice what I preach. I waited for the price to clear the 50-week Moving Average. I waited for the slope on the Moving Average to turn positive or to signal a strong Recuperation Phase.

As you can see, our reward was handsome, as the price rose from around $110 to more than $130 in a few months. But what if I had only paid attention to GLD when it traded above the 200-week Moving Average in an Accumulation Phase? First, the Recuperation Phase and the velocity of the price rise indicated that this move was for real. That gave anyone interested in buying physical gold or seeking a career within the gold industry a huge heads-up.

Doing a search for "jobs in the gold industry" yields interesting results. For instance, Barrick, a large international gold company, posted job openings all around the globe. Process manager, administrative technician, mechanic, geologist, and finance analyst are just a few examples. When you click on any of the jobs fields, it takes you to a general description, selection criteria, and a place to apply online.

For investment purposes, although the price is trading above the 200 MA, the Accumulation Phase shows a negative slope. When GLD first went into a Recuperation Phase, the gratification was instant. In the Accumulation Phase, the price sat between the 200-WMA at around $124.75 and $130.00. Although the slope on the underlying 50-WMA accelerated to the upside, the Accumulation Phase taking flight remained iffy. Therefore, the risk for anyone first buying GLD is a failure on a weekly close (meaning that by the end of the session on a Friday, the price closed under $124.75).

Gold Fails the Negatively Sloped 200-Week Moving Average

For consistency's sake, waiting for the slope on the 200-WMA to neutralize is the most conservative move. The slope of GLD continues to later in 2016. We exited the trade when GLD broke the 200-WMA in early October. Afterward, the GLD price continued to decline because the negative slope in the 200-WMA came home to roost. The 200-WMA served perfectly as the reason not to pay up and the reason to modify a bullish bias.

Homebuilders versus Real Estate 2008–2012

One aspect of real estate to think about is that of buying land and building a home versus buying new construction or an existing home. Naturally, there are other factors beyond the phase and making a sound economic decision. Personal lifestyle counts for a lot.

When my husband and I moved from Pound Ridge, New York, to Santa Fe, New Mexico, we rented for more than a year so that we could make the right decision before buying. What we knew for sure was that our incredibly busy schedule prevented us from either building or buying a fixer-upper. We needed a turnkey house. We also wanted to sell our existing home in New York before buying another one. We still pinch ourselves at how fortunate we were to sell in 2007, right before the crash!

As investors and traders, we also assessed the phases of the Homebuilders sector and the Real Estate sector. We looked at the comparison in 2008, when we bought the house in Santa Fe, to determine the best value.

The chart in figure 17.2 compares Toll Brothers (TOL), an American homebuilder, the Homebuilders ETF (XHB), and the Real Estate ETF (IYR), during an identical four-year period. Although there is not much difference among any of these charts in 2008, as pretty much everything declined, there were subtler differences as 2009 began. Even more distinctive are the differences in the charts midway through 2011 and into 2012. In 2009, all entered a Recuperation Phase. Remember, quantitative easing made the cost of borrowing money way cheaper. That helped both industries.

In the beginning of 2011, all three entered an Accumulation Phase. Other than the interest rates dropping, from what you see on the charts, building or buying (according to phases from

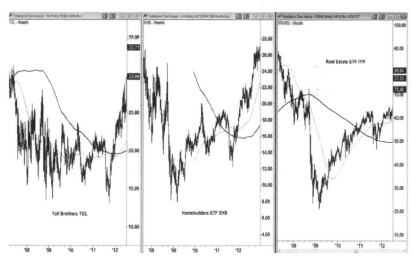

Figure 17.2. Comparing Homebuilders ETF to Real Estate ETF 2008–2012 (Courtesy of TradeStation Technologies, Inc.)

2009 to 2011) looked equally advantageous. As we get into the summer of 2011, when the market dropped after the U.S. credit rating was downgraded, Homebuilders (XHB) dropped harder and faster than Real Estate (IYR) did. Whereas Toll Brothers and Homebuilders dropped into Bearish and Distribution Phases, Real Estate held the 200-week Moving Average, entering a Caution Phase. By 2012, all entered Bullish Phases, with Toll Brothers rising precipitously.

There are many articles on the advantages and disadvantages of building versus buying a home. Bottom line—people must weigh what works best for them. Using the phases, however, you just might make a better financial decision if you can compare the two charts and assess which trend works to your benefit. In figure 17.2, that did not work out so clearly. All three entered Accumulation Phases that were weak, as shown by the downward-pointing slopes of the 200-week Moving Average.

The price rose faster in Homebuilders than in Real Estate in 2012. The cost of buying a home has fallen since the mortgage crisis in 2008. In 2012, the median price of an existing home was $177,200. The average home price was $225,800. For a new home constructed in 2012, the median price was $245,200 and the average was $292,200. We see that distinction clearly in the charts.

That Was Then, This Is Now

Had you bought an existing home in 2011–2012 versus building one, considering the near-zero interest rate, in terms of price, you still did about the same. According to the Association of Home Builders, the median price of a new home in the United States was $301,400 in February 2016, while the median price of an existing home was $212,300. That means that the cost of buying a home has risen less than $40,000, while the cost of building one has risen about $60,000 since 2012.

You know why I love phases? Instead of dissecting analysts' reports, I'd much rather look at the weekly charts. Toll Brothers is a classic example of a company that cleared into a Bullish Phase in early 2012 and had an unbelievable run-up in price until late 2015 and early 2016. TOL then languished in a Bear Phase for a year until early 2017, when it cleared back over the 200-WMA and slopes turned positive. At that point, the price of TOL's stock was $33.00. It ran up to $52.73 in a year's time.

In August 2016, the *Wall Street Journal* reported that confidence among U.S. homebuilders for the single-family home market was rising—a good sign for the economy. With the ETF XHB already in an uptrend as illustrated in figure 17.2, there was no reason to guess the future of Toll Brothers. All you need is to simply watch for a phase change to Accumulation and then to Bullish.

Why Millennials Need to Understand Phases

When I get the chance to talk with a person under the age of thirty who is willing to converse with me, I ask many questions so I may learn more about Millennials' dreams and goals for the future. Happily, many of the younger generation I talk to are extremely eager to tell me not only their thoughts on their own lives but also their fears and hopes for the planet at large.

In a discussion over lunch at a restaurant in town, I discovered that the twenty-four-year-old working the counter had built all the furniture in the restaurant. That in itself is commendable. What his accomplishment meant to him elucidated the sentiment of his generation: sustainability. As we talked further, I found out Tony was finishing school to begin a career in renewable energy. His main goal: to create sustainable greenhouses powered by renewable energy and gray water. For him, the ability to live off the grid drives his ambition.

Later in the discussion, we talked about money. Tony believes a lot of his generation is completely unrealistic about money. They believe accumulating wealth should not be a goal, or they believe that if they just imagine themselves becoming entrepreneurs, they will make it.

Tony relayed a real sense of suspicion about Wall Street and investing, accepting as true that the stock market is evil because pure capitalism does not help the ailing world. Granted, youth and idealism have gone hand in hand forever. However, as I researched further, I discovered that Tony's viewpoints are not too far off the mark from the consensus of Millennials.

According to the Harvard University Institute of Politics, less than 5 percent of Millennial voters think that reforming Wall Street is a priority. More than 30 percent, however, view improving the economy as a top priority. When I explored further, I found that "just 19 percent of voters age 18–29 describe themselves as 'capitalists' and 42 percent support capitalism."[1]

Since Tony expressed the division among his generation, I also discovered that Goldman Sachs allegedly received more than a quarter million applications from students looking for summer jobs. That was a 46 percent increase from 2012.

Furthermore, Millennials are growing 401(k)s and increasing their exposure to equities. Young workers who are automatically enrolled in 401(k)s may not even know or fully understand just how exposed they are to equities. According to recent statistics, Millennial portfolios favor equities over fixed-income investments. As long as the market is doing well, that's not a problem. However, if the market should have a sharp decline, the probability of panic selling increases. That is precisely why it is critical that if you are part of the Millennial generation, you understand your portfolio balance between fixed income and equities. Now, you can use the phases to make the necessary adjustments.

To add to the mix, 49 percent of Millennials support the idea of using companies like Apple or Google, rather than traditional financial-service companies such as Visa, which are generated from banks, to pay for consumer products. Eventually, this can have a devastating impact on big banks. Should this occur, the domino effect would not bode well for Wall Street.

Therefore, if we draw some conclusions, Millennials support social causes and want to work on Wall Street but are leery of the label "capitalist." They are heading away from traditional banking and toward online applications. Although most Millennials may be unaware of their huge equity holdings in their 401(k)s, those polled expressed only an 11 percent approval rating of Wall Street.

Socially Responsible Investing (SRI) and ETFs

In today's market, many exchange-traded funds are also known as "sustainable," "green" or "ethical." As a socially conscious generation, one can choose from a growing list of ETFs to buy and put into a portfolio. Interestingly, as I researched the history of socially responsible investing, I found that it dates back to 1758, when the Quakers prohibited members from participating in the slave trade.

By the 1960s, SRI became more popular. Martin Luther King Jr. advocated boycotting companies that harmed the progression of social causes. In turn, he encouraged investing in causes supporting civil and women's rights, plus antiwar movements.

The idea of SRI is to increase capitalization in companies that work to perpetuate social causes and improve the environment. Nevertheless, you also want to make sure that you can make money. Like any other stock, commodity, or ETF, you can monitor phases and make decisions about investments according to both your conscience and your wallet.

The number of socially responsible mutual funds is increasing. With as few as 167 in 2001, there are currently more than 500. As with any mutual fund, before placing money into one, make sure you read the prospectus so you have a clear understanding of where the fund managers invest.

Know the Phase and the Risk

Also known as ESG, or "environmental, social, and governance" (meaning corporate governance), socially conscious investing requires a bit of research. A reason why I have focused so much on ETFs is that you can buy or sell a basket of companies rather than rely on the returns of just one company. With SRI, the same applies.

Many of the ETFs I researched had already made spectacular moves and are in significant Bullish Phases. Some remain in Bearish Phases, while some are just entering Accumulation Phases. Two U.S. large-cap ETFs and extremely popular investments that track companies that have positive environmental, social, and governance qualities are iShares MSCI U.S.A. ESG (SUSA) and Social ETF DSI.

In SUSA's basket of stocks, Ecolab Inc., Microsoft Corporation, and Apple Inc. are the three heaviest weighted. That means together they make up more than 10 percent of SUSA's holdings. SUSA screens these companies to ensure their having positive environmental, social, and governance characteristics.

DSI's basket of stocks comprises socially responsible companies in the United States that also fit the ESG criteria. The biggest holding is Microsoft. Then comes Facebook, Inc., and Alphabet, Inc., Class C and Class A. Intel Corporation and Verizon make up the next two heaviest-weighted companies. The five companies combined equal more than 15 percent of the DSI basket. If you examine the dominant sectors in DSI, Information Technology makes up nearly 27 percent, with Healthcare at 14 percent and Consumer Discretionary at 13 percent.

In figure 17.3, the top right side is SUSA. In a strong Bullish Phase, buying it at the price of $91.34 shown on the current chart means you are paying up. The risk to the nearest Weekly Moving Average or the 50-WMA is far—in fact, too far. However, if the market corrects, so will SUSA. The opportunity, should the price fall to $85.00, is much better as far as risk is concerned. Remember, the risk is how much you are willing to lose. The easiest way to cal-

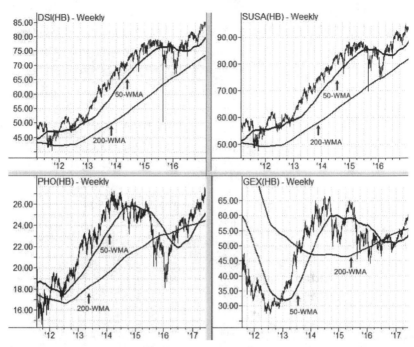

Figure 17.3. Socially Responsible Investing—2 ETFs 2012–2016/ Water and Alternative Energy ETFs 2013–2016 (Courtesy of Trade-Station Technologies, Inc.)

culate how much you might lose is to figure out how far the current price is from the closest major Moving Average. On the top left is DSI. Also in a strong Bullish Phase, its current price of $81.24 gives you a risk down to the 50-WMA at $75.68. However, each ETF may continue higher. It behooves us as investors to try to make the lowest risk investment possible and avoid those that might cost us a lot of money should the market fall. The closer the price sits to a major Moving Average, the lower the risk since the price will have the least distance to fall before you know you are wrong.

Right now you may be thinking, "But I'm dying to buy a socially conscious ETF!" You and me both! So I checked out some weekly charts. Included are two ETFs, both socially conscious, in Accumulation Phases. PHO is the ETF for PowerShares Water Resources. The basket contains companies that create products to conserve and purify water, primarily companies that exist in the United States at 95.10 percent; Brazil makes up 4.90 percent. The Industrial sector makes up 66.06 percent, and Utilities makes up 24.28 percent of PHO.

The heaviest-weighted companies are American Water Works, Danaher Corporation, Ecolab Inc., and Roper Technologies. There are thirty-six total companies in PHO's basket. PHO began 2016 in a Distribution Phase. By mid-January, the 50-WMA crossed below the 200-WMA for a death cross and entry into a Bearish Phase. By mid-March, PHO entered a Recuperation Phase. As my favorite phase, this would be the optimal time to buy—when the "smart money" gets hip to it, before the public thinks about it, and when the risk to the 50-WMA is nominal.

Nevertheless, in the beginning of June 2016, PHO crossed the 200-WMA into an Accumulation Phase. Amazingly, the slope on the 200-WMA had already turned positive. That phenomenon is rare. That means you could have bought PHO at the end of the week when the phase changed to positive and risked to (that is, exited the position) under the low price of that week—an excellent risk/reward, as we say in the trading business.

VanEck Vectors Global Alternative Energy ETF, or GEX, focuses primarily on Alternative Energy Equities. If you are like me, you believe that alternative energy industries will thrive in the future. GEX gives you exposure to solar and wind power, as well as to other renewable energy sources. The assets in GEX are 52 percent in the United States, with 48 percent of the assets represented internationally.

With thirty-three holdings, the top one is Tesla Motors with 10.31 percent. Eaton Corp. PLC is next with 10.17 percent, followed by Vestas Wind Systems A/S with 9.96 percent. First Solar, Inc., and Cree, Inc., together make up about another 10.5 percent.

Similar to PHO, GEX fell into a Distribution Phase in early 2016. The first week in June, GEX had a death cross and entered a Bearish Phase. But that phase was short-lived. By the last week in June, the price rose into a Recuperation Phase, crossing the neutrally sloped 50-week Moving Average. Is it a good time to buy? Absolutely.

Then, one week later, GEX crossed the 200-WMA into an Accumulation Phase. At the time of writing, when I captured a screenshot of the weekly chart, GEX sat on the 200-WMA. This is an excellent buy opportunity.

I'm Not Ready to Invest Yet, but . . .

Let's say you love the idea of investing in an SRI but need to wait. Perhaps you must wait because you have to accumulate enough money or you need to open an account or talk to your financial planner. If that describes you, here's a great opportunity waiting to happen in alternative energy.

The Guggenheim Solar ETF (TAN) targets the solar power energy industry. TAN has twenty-three holdings. In the sector breakdown, Renewable Energy technology makes up 67.09 percent, with 49.25 percent of the asset allocation in the U.S. stock market versus 50 percent allocated internationally.

The top five weighted companies at the time of writing are First Solar, Inc., Solaredge Technologies Inc., Sunrun Inc., and Xinyi Solar Holdings, Ltd. Together those companies make up nearly 30 percent of TAN's holdings. As of July 2018, TAN was in a Bearish Phase. That makes the decision easy. Once it clears into a Recuperation Phase with a positive slope on the 50-WMA, it could be the beginning of beautiful investment and career opportunities.

In other chapters, I demonstrated how useful the charts and phases are in making career and educational choices. The same is true for socially responsible investing. As Millennials are focusing more on social and environmental ways to tackle major societal issues, the phases of both the ETFs and individual companies can help lead them in the right direction.

What about Big Banks?

Millennials, credited with leading a financial revolution, want banks to provide mobile access to their accounts. Since the statistics show that Millennials visit bank branches less and access computers more than their predecessors did, big banks must keep up in order to stay alive. "A project called the Millennial Disruption Index, reported that banks are not only among the most unlikable brands with this demographic, but one-third of those surveyed believed they would not need a bank at all in the future."[2]

The three biggest banks in the United States, as measured by assets under management and market capitalization (the total dollar market value of a company's outstanding shares), are, in order, J. P. Morgan Chase & Co., Bank of America, and Wells Fargo. Citigroup Inc. runs neck and neck with Wells Fargo. Combined, their total assets equal approximately $7.5 trillion.

By the end of 2016, the three banks' charts (figure 17.4) illustrated two different phases. J. P. Morgan Chase & Co. (JPM) and Bank of America (BAC) were in Accumulation Phases. Wells Fargo was in a Caution Phase. It is fascinating that the order of assets

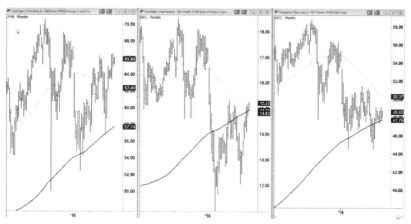

Figure 17.4. Big Banks J. P. Morgan, Bank of America, Wells Fargo 2016

under management (AUM) appears to dictate the strength of the phase, with JPM leading in both.

While difficult at that point to draw any substantial conclusion for the future, it appeared safe to say that the diversion among the phases was noteworthy. For potential investment opportunities, I interpret the disparity as either a great buy opportunity in the laggards or a great short opportunity in JPM.

It turned out to be a great buy opportunity in the laggards. By July 2018, JPM traded up to $120 before falling back to $110. BAC traded up to $33.00 at its peak, and WFC, the weakest still, traded up to $66.31 before retreating down to $56.00. More important, the phases told you to buy. In two years, all three stocks nearly doubled in price.

Considering the articles I've read about Millennials and the future of big banks, along with current data, the future remains in the future and clearly not what we see in the present phase environment. All three banks as of July 2018 were in weekly Bullish Phases. Should any or all enter Caution Phases, you know what to do.

Using the Megatrends in an Accumulation Phase

Earlier in this book, I wrote about megatrends in other phases. Some of those trends are continuations of ones that had already started and could continue. Others are ones that I consider in "infancy" or just beginning. Still others, after years of moving in one direction, might run out of steam and have an abrupt reversal in trend.

Walking the walk, phases are my clearest, simplest, and lowest-risk way of timing investments. The timing of other decisions like education or careers, where risk may not be as relevant, does not diminish the importance of seeing a new phase begin or end. It is always better to have the time to make plans early and have an advantage over the competition.

My Top Ten Megatrends to Watch

1. Climate Change—When will alternative energy replace coal and oil?

2. Geopolitical Turmoil—Will world disorder intensify?

3. Social Media—Which applications grow in popularity and monetize as well?

4. Online Shopping versus Brick-and-Mortar—Will the mall be able to keep up?

5. Growing Number of Millennial Investors—What trends will they follow?

6. Video Gaming—Will the fifteen-year trend continue to grow?

7. Smart TVs versus Cable Providers—Will cable become obsolete?

8. 3-D Printing—A trend in infancy, when will printers become cost-effective?

9. Medical and Recreational Marijuana Use—Will legalization continue to spread?

10. Alternative Currency and Block Chain Technology—Will it replace the dollar?

Some of these trends have occurred for years, while others have yet to get going. For example, social media, online shopping, and video gaming all have mature trends. 3-D printing, by contrast, has yet to catch fire. Alternative Currencies ignited in 2017, only to decline in 2018. Unfortunately, geopolitical turmoil experienced a surge in the last few years, especially at the start of 2016.

For the purpose of this chapter, let's focus on the Accumulation Phase.

Previously, I pointed out the Solar ETF TAN. That's one to keep an eye out for, as a Bearish Phase can become a Recuperation Phase and then improve to an Accumulation Phase. For climate change—politically a hot topic—solar energy, particularly First Solar Corporation, is in a Caution Phase along with GEX (Global Alternative Energy).

Flipping through the charts of so many names associated with the megatrends, I realize that the weekly phases established themselves long before writing this book. I literally checked both ETFs and stocks in each trend.

Besides the extraordinary lag in solar energy and 3-D printing compared to online shopping companies like Amazon, or social media companies like Facebook and video gaming stocks like ACTi Vision, some of the other key stocks or ETFs do not have enough data to assess the weekly phase. For example, HACK, the ETF that tracks companies actively involved in providing cyber security technology and services, began trading in November 2014.

The weekly chart on HACK does not have enough data to show either the 50- or the 200-week Moving Averages. However, if we switch to a daily chart, the 50- and 200-day Moving Averages show

Figure 17.5. Cyber Security ETF HACK Daily Chart November 2015–October 2017 (Courtesy of TradeStation Technologies, Inc.)

up. In the fall of 2017, the phase on the daily chart was decidedly Bullish.

What should weekly phase followers do if the charts are too new to show enough data? There are a couple of choices. One has the option of looking at the daily chart. The 50- and 200-day Moving Averages work exactly the same way as the 50- and 200-week Moving Averages. The phases are the same for each.

For this book, we have used Weekly Moving Averages because the phase changes happen more slowly. There is less volatility. The ability to see longer-term phase changes increases, enabling you to make better longer-term investment and life decisions. As with a Bullish Phase on a weekly chart, the price as of August 2016 showed the risk too great if one were thinking about buying this ETF. The distance between the 50-day Moving Average (DMA) and the price is significant. A correction back down to the 50 DMA would cost a lot of money.

According to the daily chart since early 2016, the phase changed from Bearish to Recuperation in March. In July, the phase changed to Accumulation. In late July, when the 50 crossed back above the 200 DMA, the phase turned Bullish. As this chapter features the Accumulation Phase, see how the momentum on HACK increased exponentially once it entered the Accumulation Phase. That represents the ideal Accumulation Phase—when buying accumulates, the risk to the 200 DMA is close and low and the price then rises rapidly.

Another option is to look at the top five to ten holdings of any ETF and then check out the weekly chart on any of those companies. In HACK, as of July 2018, the top five holdings were Qualys, Inc.; Palo Alto Networks, Inc.; Impreva, Inc.; Check Point Software, Inc.; and Cisco Systems. Holdings and their weight in any ETF basket may change according to a stock's price, a merger or acquisition of a stock, or some other criteria the ETF originator creates.

The megatrends work really well in helping establish which areas to look at for investments. Nevertheless, not all of the megatrends measure potential growth. Some rely on failure. Take the megatrend example of online shopping versus brick-and-mortar. Amazon, the kingpin of online shopping, has continually rallied since 2015. Meanwhile, brick-and-mortar companies such as Macy's, Inc. (M), dramatically fell in price since it peaked in mid-2015.

How Do I Use This Information?

Whether you make your own list of megatrends you wish to track, read the predictions of your own favorite gurus, or follow the ones I am looking at, the phases tell you a lot about when to buy and when to sell.

The same principles apply for making educational or continuing-education decisions. If the phase is in Recuperation, Accumulation, or Bullish, most likely the area is one of growth. If the phase is in Caution, Distribution, or Bearish, that area could be ripe for contraction. The same applies to career changes. You can watch different sectors, such as Cyber Security, Retail, Real Estate, Solar Energy, and so on, for opportunities. You can also track the top companies that each of those sector ETFs hold in their basket of stocks.

Summary

1. The Accumulation Phase is a confirmation that the Recuperation Phase is real.

2. Typically, the Accumulation Phase requires patience. Although "smart money" begins to buy during the Accumulation Phase, oftentimes it does so with a willingness to wait years, if necessary, for the price to increase.

3. Millennials, as the fastest-growing population of investors, in particular need to understand phases.

4. As Millennials become more interested in sustainability, socially responsible investing in ETFs offers great opportunities. On the other side, the changing landscape in other areas, such as banking, offers other types of investments.

5. Megatrends that have occurred over years or are just starting to emerge offer an excellent road map of stocks and ETFs to follow and watch for phase changes. The Accumulation Phase can be a great time to see big shifts in momentum for investing and making major personal financial decisions.

CONCLUSION

W hen I first began to write this book, the S&P 500 was in a strong Bullish Phase. From January 2015 until July 2015, SPY had a positive slope in both the 50- and the 200-WMA, with the price well above both Moving Averages.

In August 2015, the price fell beneath the 50-WMA, giving SPY and investors fair warning of what was to come. The price had one brief stint back above the 50-WMA in the autumn of 2015, which calmed some nerves; however, the slope on the 50-WMA did not recover. From July until December, the slope appeared flat to slightly negative.

In early 2016, SPY and most of the entire market fell hard. Yet it never broke below the 200-WMA. Furthermore, SPY never deteriorated in phase beyond Caution. In fact, by April 2016, SPY returned to a Bullish Phase. And the slope in the 50-WMA was positive as 2016 ended. As of August 2018, SPY continued to sit in a strong Bullish Phase.

What does that potentially set up?

To date, SPY has not closed out a week below the 50-WMA since March 2016. Looking ahead, should SPY fail the 50-WMA and enter a new Caution Phase, I would take that for what it's worth: a warning. Should SPY break the 200-WMA and go into a

Distribution Phase, take heed. After all, the last time SPY entered a Bearish Phase was in October 2009. And we *all* know how that worked out for the market!

Now that you have a visual and succinct way to "read" the phases in the market indices or any sector or stock, this should not happen to you. Additionally, you have the reliable group of the six main economic sectors to keep track of. Watch how they behave individually and as a group. Think about what each one means for the economy. Remember, the sectors united are powerful. However, if the sectors divide, they are equally powerful. Both scenarios give you more than enough information to make smart decisions about your family's future and finances.

Predictions for the Next Ten Years

Research Affiliates, an investment advisory firm, did an analysis in October 2016 on the likelihood of mainstream investors making money in the market over the next ten years. The average portfolio holds a blend of 60 percent stocks and 40 percent bonds. Based on what they call "a full distribution of possible future outcomes," they predict the average portfolio will have 0 percent probability of making an annualized return of 5 percent or more over the next ten years.

The research goes on to say that a more diversified portfolio that holds non-U.S. assets, both large- and small-cap equities, plus other atypical instruments, such as emerging market equities, will fare a bit better. They see that setup as having a 2.3–7 percent chance of getting more than 5 percent annualized real returns in the next ten years.

Naturally, the researchers provide the data with the caveat that "perfect foresight eludes" them. "Perfect foresight" eludes everyone. The phases, however, do not require foresight beyond one's ability to read a weekly chart and see which phase any instrument is in at the time.

Want to diversify your portfolio?

Look for indices, emerging markets, commodities, U.S. small- and large-cap companies, and ETFs that are in the Recuperation, Accumulation, or Bullish Phases to buy. Avoid, liquidate, or short instruments that are in Caution, Distribution, or Bearish Phases. Do not rely on the media or anyone else to direct where your money goes *without* consulting the phases. You have a compass. Not everyone does. You have a basis of knowledge. Not everybody does. You have a guide for the six phases and the six economic sectors. Not everybody does.

The biggest headline of 2017: "The 45th President of the United States . . . Now the World Holds Its Breath."[1]

What Will Happen Next?

To help you "see" the future of the U.S. economy, all you need to do is watch the economic sectors and the phase each one is in, and the divergence among the sectors will help you gauge which sectors of the economy should benefit and which ones will not. Furthermore, as we learned earlier, the future bodes better for a family united than it does for one divided.

The Era of Fake News

Fabricated or fake news intends to mislead or deceive, and it lacks a basis in facts. Ramses the Great began fake news for political gain in 1200 BC. In the present day, the expression "fake news" has become widespread. Undoubtedly, news, whether real or fake, influences the stock market.

I hope that you have learned from this book how to tune out the noise and why you should pay attention to the phases. Dispassionate investing, regardless of current events, empowers you to make intelligent decisions about how to spend, save, or invest your money. You can now make sound life decisions for you and your family. Enjoy!

ACKNOWLEDGMENTS

I dedicate this book to all of you who read my daily blog, attend my webinars, subscribe to my premium service ("Mish's Market Minute Advantage"), and interact with me on social media.

I have written millions of words throughout the years. Yet putting those words cohesively into a book takes a "village." I extend my gratitude to the long list of friends, family, coworkers, partners, and loved ones who have helped, encouraged, and inspired me.

First, thanks to the special and regular education teachers, lawyers, and school administrators who believed I could modify all general education curricula so that every student could have successful access to full inclusion.

Paul Sarnoff—author, commodities analyst, and former director of research at Conticommodity Services, Inc., from 1976 to 1982—launched my career in finance. Mr. Sarnoff hired me to work for Conti Commodities as a floor analyst on the Sugar, Coffee and Cocoa Exchange. May he rest in peace.

During my years as an independent floor trader on the commodities exchanges at the World Trade Center, other seasoned floor brokers and traders took me under their wing. Too numerous to mention individually, please accept a resounding shout-out of appreciation to my many mentors on the Floor from 1980 until 1993.

In 2009, after the mortgage crisis, Geoff Bysshe, current president of Dataview, LLC, and longtime friend, recommended that I return to finance to work for MarketGauge as the director of education and research. My deepest thanks go to him and the entire support staff of MarketGauge.

Sarah Lovett, author, writing coach, and friend, helped me identify and organize the steps I needed to start the book.

Physics became a focus while writing about phases. I thank my nephew Jim Wolongevicz, an engineer working with advanced optical and experimental satellite systems with the air force, for providing me with invaluable insight and explanation.

Thank you, Robert Flenner and James Kimball, for spending hours creating the charts.

The number of willing beta readers is humbling. I wish to thank Elnora Williams, James Kimball, Jeff Brown, Jennifer Graves, Barbara Cranner, Alex Hill, Mary Guernsey, Nadine Donovan, Roberta Binkley, PhD, Robert Christie, PhD, and Boris Palanov for taking the time to read the beta copy and offer their invaluable feedback.

Huge thanks to Cynde Christie, my editor. The title "editor" does not describe half of the help she provided me through the entire process. I could not have done this book without her extraordinary dedication, insights, and talent.

I'm so grateful for my mom, Betty Cohen. Her unconditional love and support have kept me feeling positive for my entire life.

Last but not least, I cannot imagine life without my husband, Keith Schneider. He's my everything—cheerleader, rock, teacher, best friend, partner, and lover. Thanks for always standing right by my side.

HOW CAN WE HELP?

O ur website at www.marketgauge.com has a significant amount of free data available. There are also other online services and outlets that provide free data.

Under the tab "Market Beat," you will find my *Mish's Daily* and my husband Keith Schneider's (CEO of MarketGauge) "Weekly Market Outlook," plus videos and commentary by Geoff Bysshe, president of MarketGauge. Our educational courses and trading services are listed under "Products and Services."

You can follow me on twitter: @marketminute. Our Facebook page is MarketGauge.com.

Please feel free to email me at mish@marketgauge.com. For more information about our Registered Investment Advisory Firm, go to www.mgamllc.com.

Market Phases

```
                    ┌─────────────┐
                    │   Bullish   │
                    │ = Euphoria  │
                    └─────────────┘
  ┌──────────────┐                  ┌──────────────┐
  │ Accumulation │                  │   Caution    │
  │ = Optimism   │                  │  = Anxiety   │
  └──────────────┘                  └──────────────┘
  ┌──────────────┐                  ┌──────────────┐
  │ Recuperation │                  │ Distribution │
  │   = Hope     │                  │   = Fear     │
  └──────────────┘                  └──────────────┘
                    ┌─────────────┐
                    │   Bearish   │
                    │ = Despair   │
                    └─────────────┘
```

Bullish Phase

The 50-WMA > the 200-WMA.

The slope on the 50-WMA should be positive, with the 200 neutral to positive.

The price is > both the 50- and the 200-WMA.

Caution Phase

The 50-WMA > 200-WMA.

The slope on the 50-WMA is starting to flatten or turn slightly negative. The slope on the 200-WMA usually remains positive.

The price is < the 50-WMA but > the 200-WMA.

Distribution Phase

The 50-WMA is > the 200-WMA.

The slope on the 50-WMA usually goes from neutral to declining. The 200-WMA might also be declining in slope.

The price is < both the 50- and the 200-WMA.

Bearish Phase

The 50-WMA is < 200-WMA.

The slope on the 50-WMA is negative. The slope on the 200-WMA has neutralized and is starting to turn negative.

The price is < both the 50- and the 200-WMA.

Recuperation Phase

The 50-WMA is < 200-WMA.

The slope on the 50-WMA should begin to neutralize or start to turn positive, while the 200-WMA slope remains negative. That will take longer to stop its decline.

The price is > the 50-WMA, yet < 200-WMA. The closer the price is to the 50-WMA, the better the risk should the phase fail.

Accumulation Phase

The 50-WMA is < the 200-WMA.

The slope on the 50-WMA is positive. The slope on the 200-WMA is beginning to neutralize after a long pe-riod of having a negative slope.

The price is > both the 50- and the 200-WMA.

6 KEY TERMS DEFINED

The Economic Sectors—Represent one stock index (the Russell 2000) and five economic sectors (Retail, Semiconductors, Transportation, Regional Banks, and Biotechnology) that offer a broad-based glimpse into how the U.S. economy is doing.

Exchange-Traded Fund (ETF)—A security that tracks an index, a commodity, bonds, or a basket of assets like an index fund. Investors buy and sell ETFs like a common stock on a stock exchange.

Index (indices)—A stock *index* or stock market *index* is a measurement of the value of a section of the stock market, computed from the prices of selected stocks (typically a weighted average). It is a tool used by investors and *financial* managers to describe the market and to compare the return on specific investments.

Market Phase—Market phases help to describe an instrument's strength or weakness. Instruments move from one phase to another, based on how the Moving Averages are stacked and sloped and where the price is in relation to the Moving Averages.

Simple Moving Average—A Simple Moving Average (SMA) is the average of a stock's closing prices (minute, hour, day, week, or month) over a certain period of time. Unlike an exponential moving average, which gives more weight to the most recent days, the same weight is given to each day while calculating the average for a Simple Moving Average. The shorter-term SMAs are faster to respond to market action than the longer-term SMAs. When you hear the term "Moving Average," it usually refers to SMAs. For this book, I primarily use a 50-week and a 200-week Moving Average.

Technical Analysis—A means of examining and predicting price movements in the financial markets, based on an asset's chart history. Analysts use a wide range of tools to find trends and patterns on charts such as Moving Averages, support, and resistance levels.

NOTES

Chapter One

1. Stan Weinstein, *Stan Weinstein's Secrets for Profiting in Bull and Bear Markets* (Burr Ridge, IL: Dow Jones-Irwin, 1988).
2. Chuck Dukas and T. Parker Gallagher, *The TRENDadvisor Guide to Breakthrough Profits: A Proven System for Building Wealth in the Financial Markets* (Hoboken, NJ: John C. Wiley & Sons, 2006).
3. William O'Neil, *How to Make Money Selling Stocks Short* (Hoboken, NJ: John C. Wiley & Sons, 2005).

Chapter Two

1. George E. P. Box and Gwilym M. Jenkins, *Time Series Analysis: Forecasting and Control*, rev. ed. (San Francisco, CA: Holden-Day, 1976), iix.
2. James Cunningham and Norman Herr, *Hands-on Physics Acitivities with Real Life Applications* (San Francisco, CA: Jossey-Bass, 1994), 304–6.

Chapter Three

1. Neil Irwin and David Cho, "Markets in Disarray as Lending Locks Up," *Washington Post*, September 18, 2008.
2. Daniel Gross, "Why the Economy Is Showing Green Shoots," *Newsweek*, April 17, 2009.

3. Alex Crippen, "Warren Buffett's Live Lunch Interview on CNBC with Becky Quinn Reported by Alex Crippen," CNN, June 24, 2009.

4. Bradley Klontz and Sonya Britt, "Financial Trauma: Why the Abandonment of Buy-and-Hold in Favor of Tactical Asset Management May Be a Symptom of Post-Traumatic Stress," *Journal of Financial Therapy* 3, no. 2 (2012): 14–27.

5. Klontz and Britt, "Financial Trauma."

Chapter Four

1. Brad Comincioli, "The Stock Market as a Leading Indicator: An Application of Granger Causality," *University Avenue Undergraduate Journal of Economics* 1, no. 1 (1996).

Chapter Five

1. Peter Lynch, *One Up on Wall Street: How to Use What You Already Know to Make Money in the Market*, 2nd ed. (New York: Simon & Schuster, 2000).

Chapter Seven

1. Suze Orman, "10 Tips to Spring Clean Your Finances," *Suze Orman* (blog), March 23, 2015, https://www.suzeorman.com/blog/suze-ormans-10-tips-to-spring-clean-your-finances.

Chapter Eight

1. Michael S. Wogalter, "Technology Will Revolutionize Warnings," NCSU Psychology Department Proceedings of the Solutions in Safety through Technology Symposium 2006—American Society of Safety Engineers, 2006.

Chapter Nine

1. Council of Economic Advisers, "10 Economic Facts about Millennials," October 15, 2014, https://www.businessinsider.com/10-economic-facts-about-millennials-2014-10.

2. Council of Economic Advisers, "10 Economic Facts."

3. Ranker.com. "Listopedia. Science & Medicine," 2009, http://www.ranker.com/fact-lists/companies/industry.

4. Council of Economic Advisers, *15 Economic Facts about Millennials* (Washington, DC: Council of Economic Advisers, Executive Office of the President, 2014).

5. Divya Raghavan, "How Student Loans Affect Your Credit Score," *U.S. News & World Report*, July 7, 2014.

Chapter Eleven

1. Colbourne College, "Business Environment," n.d., http://colbourne college.weebly.com/uploads/2/3/7/9/23793496/2.2_-_fiscal.pdf.

2. Paul A. Volcker, "The Role of Central Banks," Federal Reserve Bank of Kansas City, 1990, https://www.kansascityfed.org/publicat/sym pos/1990/S90VOLCK.pdf.

3. Tara Siegel Bernard, "Medical, Dental, 401(k)? Now Add School Loan Aid to Job Benefits," *New York Times*, March 25, 2016.

4. Tony Robbins, *Money Master the Game: 7 Simple Steps to Financial Freedom* (New York: Simon & Schuster, 2014).

5. Robbins, *Money Master the Game*.

6. Suze Orman, "Suze Orman's 10 Tips for a Fresh Financial Start," *O: The Oprah Magazine* (January 2009).

7. Suzanne Woolley, "Wanted: Big Returns, Low Risk. (And Millennials? They Want *10.2%*)," Bloomberg.com, June 16, 2016, https://www.bloomberg.com/news/articles/2016-06-16/wanted-big-returns-low-risk-and-millennials-they-want-10-2.

Chapter Twelve

1. Chuck Dukas and T. Parker Gallagher, *The TRENDadvisor Guide to Breakthrough Profits: A Proven System for Building Wealth in the Financial Markets* (Hoboken, NJ: John C. Wiley & Sons, 2006).

Chapter Thirteen

1. Anna Louie Sussman and Eric Morath, "Lower Gas Prices Yield Uneven Benefits," *Wall Street Journal*, September 4, 2015.

2. Jeremy Rifkin, *The Third Industrial Revolution* (New York: St. Martin's Press, 2011).

3. Rifkin, *The Third Industrial Revolution*.

4. Drew Voros, "XOP: SPDR S&P Oil & Gas Exploration & Production," n.d., ETF.com, http://www.etf.com/XOP.

5. Russell Heimlich, "Tattooed Gen Nexters," Pew Research Center FactTank, December 9, 2008, http://www.pewresearch.org/fact-tank/2008/12/09/tattooed-gen-nexters/.

Chapter Fourteen

1. Stefan Gleason, "Peak Gold and Silver May Have Come and Gone," *Money Metals News Service*, January 21, 2016.

2. Marcy Nichalson and Clare Denina, "Gold Surges to 1-Year High on Financial Uncertainty," Reuters, February 11, 2016, https://www.reuters.com/article/us-global-precious/gold-surges-to-1-year-high-on-financial-uncertainty-idUSKCN0VK1YA.

3. Nicholson and Denina, "Gold Surges to 1-Year High on Financial Uncertainty."

Chapter Fifteen

1. Benjamin Franklin, *The Works of Benjamin Franklin*, 12 vols., edited by John Bigelow (New York: G. P. Putnam's Sons, 1817, 1904).

2. Tali Sharot, "The Optimism Bias," *Time*, May 28, 2011.

3. Mark Ragins, MD, *A Road to Recovery* (Los Angeles: Mental Health America of Los Angeles, 2016).

4. Derek Thompson, "Why Don't Americans Save More Money?" *The Atlantic*, April 19, 2016.

5. Thompson, "Why Don't Americans Save More Money?"

6. Thompson, "Why Don't Americans Save More Money?"

7. Charles Bilello, "Defense Wins Championships: The Defensive Sector Anomaly," *Pension Partners: The ATAC Rotation Manager*, September 9, 2014.

8. Charles V. Bilello and Michael A. Gayed, *An Intermarket Approach to Beta Rotation: The Strategy, Signal and Power of Utilities* (New York: Pension Partners, 2014).

Chapter Sixteen

1. Doreen Virtue, *Angel Number 101: The Meaning of 111, 123, 444 and Other Number Sequences* (London: Hay House, 2008).

Chapter 17

1. Paul Bedard, "Harvard Poll: Millennials Reject Capitalism, Media, Wall Street," *Washington Examiner*, April 25, 2016.

2. Bryan Yurcan, "What Do Millennials Want from Banks? Everything. Nothing. Whatever," *American Banker*, March 16, 2016.

Conclusion

1. "The 45th President of the United States . . . Now the World Holds Its Breath," *Daily Mirror*, January 20, 2017.

BIBLIOGRAPHY

Bedard, Paul. "Harvard Poll: Millennials Reject Capitalism, Media, Wall Street." *Washington Examiner*, April 25, 2016.

Bernard, Tara Siegal. "Medical, Dental, 401K? Now Add School Loan Aid to Job Benefits." *New York Times*, March 25, 2016.

Bilello, Charles. "Defense Wins Championships: The Defensive Sector Anomaly." *Pension Partners: The ATAC Rotation Manager*, September 9, 2014.

Bilello, Charles V., and Michael A. Gayed. *An Intermarket Approach to Beta Rotation: The Strategy, Signal and Power of Utilities.* New York: Pension Partners, 2014.

Box, George E. P., and Gwilym M. Jenkins. *Time Series Analysis: Forecasting and Control* (revised edition), iix. San Francisco, CA: Holden-Day, 1976.

Colbourne College. "Business Environment." n.d. http://colbournecollege. weebly.com/uploads/2/3/7/9/23793496/2.2_-_fiscal.pdf.

Comincioli, Brad. "The Stock Market as a Leading Indicator: An Application of Granger Causality." *University Avenue Undergraduate Journal of Economics 1*, no. 1 (1996).

Council of Economic Advisers. "10 Economic Facts about Millennials." October 15, 2014. https://www.businessinsider.com/10-economic-facts-about-millennials-2014-10.

———. *15 Economic Facts about Millennials.* Washington, DC: Council of Economic Advisers, Executive Office of the President, 2014.

Crippen, Alex. "Warren Buffett's Live Lunch Interview on CNBC with Becky Quinn Reported by Alex Crippen." CNN, June 24, 2009.

Cunningham, James, and Norman Herr. *Hands-On Physics Activities with Real Life Applications*. San Francisco, CA: Jossey-Bass, 1994.

Dukas, Chuck, and T. Parker Gallagher. *The TRENDadvisor Guide to Breakthrough Profits: A Proven System for Building Wealth in the Financial Markets*. Hoboken, NJ: John C. Wiley & Sons, 2006.

Franklin, Benjamin. *The Works of Benjamin Franklin*. 12 vols. Edited by John Bigelow. New York: G. P. Putnam's Sons, 1817, 1904.

Garver, Abe. "Abe Garver." *Forbes*, February 29, 2016.

Gleason, Stefan. "Peak Gold and Silver May Have Come and Gone." *Money Metals News Service*, January 21, 2016.

Gross, Daniel. "Why the Economy Is Showing Green Shoots." *Newsweek*, April 17, 2009.

Hay, W. W., and C. Frank Allen. *Practical Guide to Railway Engineering*. Lanham, MD: Arema, the American Railway Engineering and Maintenance of Way Association, 2003.

Heimlich, Russell. "Tattooed Gen Nexters." Pew Research Center FactTank, December 9, 2008. http://www.pewresearch.org/fact-tank/2008/12/09/tattooed-gen-nexters/.

Irwin, Neil, and David Cho. "Markets in Disarray as Lending Locks Up." *Washington Post*, September 18, 2008.

Klontz, Bradley T., and Sonya L. Britt. "Financial Trauma: Why the Abandonment of Buy-and-Hold in Favor of Tactical Asset Management May Be a Symptom of Post-Traumatic Stress." *Journal of Financial Therapy* 3, no. 2 (2012).

Lynch, Peter. *One Up on Wall Street*. 2nd ed. New York: Simon & Schuster, 2000.

Manyika, James, Michael Chui, Jacquie Bughin, Richard Dobbs, Peter Bisson, and Alex Marrs. *Institute Disruptive Technologies: Advances That Will Transform Life, Business and the Global Economy*. New York: McKinsey & Company, McKinsey Global Institute, 2013.

Newton, Sir Isaac. "Laws of Motion—Real-Life Applications." Science Clarified.com, n.d. http://www.scienceclarified.com/everday/Real-Life-Chemistry-Vol-3-Physics-Vol-1/Laws-of-Motion-life-applications.html.

Nicholson, Marcy, and Clara Denina. "Gold Surges to 1-Year High on Financial Uncertainty." Reuters, February 11, 2016. https://www. reuters.com/article/us-global-precious/gold-surges-to-1-year-high-on-financial-uncertainty-idUSKCN0VK1YA.

O'Neil, William. *How to Make Money Selling Stocks Short*. Hoboken, NJ: John C. Wiley, 2005.

Orman, Suze. "10 Tips to Spring Clean Your Finances." *Suze Orman* (blog), March 23, 2015. https://www.suzeorman.com/blog/suze-ormans-10-tips-to-spring-clean-your-finances.

———. "Suze Orman's 10 Tips for a Fresh Financial Start." *O: The Oprah Magazine* (January 2009).

Rader's Physics4Kids.com. "Newton's Laws of Motion." n.d. http://www. physics4kids.com/files/motion_laws.html.

Raghavan, Divya. "How Student Loans Affect Your Credit Score." *U.S. News & World Report*, July 7, 2014.

Ragins, Mark, MD. *A Road to Recovery*. Los Angeles: Mental Health America of Los Angeles, 2016.

Ranker.com. "Listopedia: Science & Medicine." 2009. http://www.ranker .com/fact-lists/companies/industry.

Rifkin, Jeremy. *The Third Industrial Revolution*. New York: St. Martin's Press, 2011.

Robbins, Tony. *Money Master the Game*. New York: Simon & Schuster, 2014.

Sharot, Tali. "The Optimism Bias." *Time*, May 28, 2011. http://content .time.com/time/health/article/0,8599,2074067,00.html.

"Simple Moving Average—SMA." *Investopedia*, n.d. http://www.investope dia.com/terms/s/sma.asp.

Stelter, Brian. "Disney Stock Hit By ESPN Fears." *CNN Money*, August 5, 2015.

Sussman, Anna Louie, and Eric Morath. "Lower Gas Prices Yield Uneven Benefits." *Wall Street Journal*, September 4, 2015.

Thompson, Derek. "Why Don't Americans Save More Money?" *The Atlantic*, April 19, 2016.

Tobin, James. *The Concise Encyclopedia of Economics*. Carmel, NJ: Liberty Fund, 2008.

Virtue, Doreen. *Angel Number 101: The Meaning of 111, 123, 444 and Other Number Sequences*. London: Hay House, 2008.

Volcker, Paul. "The Role of Central Banks." Federal Reserve Bank of Kansas City, 1990. http://www.kansascityfed.org/publicat/sympos/1990/S90VOLCK.pdf.

Voros, Drew. "XOP: SPDR S&P Oil & Gas Exploration & Production." ETF.com, n.d. http://www.etf.com/XOP.

Weinstein, Stan. *Stan Weinstein's Secrets for Profiting in Bull and Bear Markets.* Burr Ridge, IL: Dow Jones-Irwin, 1988.

Wogalter, Michael S. "Technology Will Revolutionize Warnings." NCSU Psychology Department Proceedings of the Solutions in Safety through Technology Symposium 2006—American Society of Safety Engineers, 2006.

Woolley, Suzanne. "Wanted: Big Returns, Low Risk." Bloomberg.com, June 16, 2016. https://www.bloomberg.com/news/articles/2016-06-16/wanted-big-returns-low-risk-and-millennials-they-want-10-2.

Yurcan, Bryan. "What Do Millennials Want from Banks? Everything. Nothing. Whatever." *American Banker*, March 16, 2016.

INDEX

PLANT YOUR MONEY TREE

*The TRENDadvisor Guide to
Breakthrough Profits* (Dukas), 7
trends: for 401(k), 62; in
biotechnology, 67–70, 190;
in bull markets, 23–24, *24*,
51–59, *52*, *54*, *58*, 61–71, *64*,
70, 107–8; in careers, 62–63; in
Distribution Phases, 110–11;
in economic sectors, 110; in
GDP, 126; geometry for, 123,
185; golden crosses for, 57–59,
58; in health care, *70*, 70–71; in
interest rates, 61–62, 140–41;
in IT, 182–83; megatrends,
47–49, *48*, 181–82, 211–16,
213; news and, 53–54, 76–77,
163–64; in oil, 134–36, *135*;
in prices, 31; psychology of,
17–19, *18*, 55–56; in real estate,
25–26; in Recuperation Phases,
144; in retail, 148; in Russell
2000 index, 103–4, *104*; science
of, 10–14; in semiconductors,
63–67, *64*; in shopping, 45; in
stock indexes, 100–101; in stock
market, 9–10; trading on, 36;
volatility, 85, 109; in WMA,
15–17
"The Twitter Accounts Investors
Need to Follow" (Kollmeyer), 4

unemployment, 97
United Parcel Service (UPS), 122
United States (U.S.): banking
in, 27–28; biotechnology in,
69–70; BLS, 35; debt ceilings
in, 191–92; dollar in, 139–42;

140; economic sectors in, 7, 26,
63–67, *64*, 79, 81–82, 133–34,
141–42, 174–75; education
in, 71; FDIC in, 123; GDP
in, 32–33; health care in, 34;
Millennials in, 92–94; QE in,
59, 115–18, 166, 176, 190–92;
stock market in, 2, 31–32;
unemployment in, 97
United States Oil Fund (USO),
134–36, *135*
UPS. *See* United Parcel Service
USO. *See* United States Oil Fund
utilities, 178–83, *179*

Vanguard, 175
Virtue, Doreen, 186–87
volatility, 85, 109
Volcker, Paul, 118, 192
volume, 14

Wall Street. *See* institutional
investors
Wal-Mart, 89–92, *91*, 168
Weekly Moving Average
(WMA), 3, 7, 12, 229–30; in
Accumulation Phases, 187–90,
188; in bear markets, 25–26,
44; in bull markets, *75*, 75–76,
178; in Caution Phases, 168;
for DISH Network, 78, *78*;
education of, 14–15, *15*,
20–21; for financial planners,
6–7; institutional investors
and, 19–20; for knowledge,
9–10, 226–27; market phases
and, 45–46, *46*, 150, 153–54,

217–18; as news, 130; prices and, 10–11, *11*; psychology of, 52–53, 121; for real estate, *54*, 54–55; for Recuperation Phases, 135, 161–65, *162*; for retail, 106–7; in Russell 2000 index, 74, 89; slope in, 137–38, *188*, 188–89; for S&P 500 index, 56–57, 130–31, *131*; in stock market, 3; in technical analysis, 10–14, 17–19, *18*, 29, 65; trends in, 15–17. *See also* death crosses; golden crosses

Weinstein, Stan, 6–7

Wells Fargo, *210*, 210–11

Whole Foods, 42–44

WMA. *See* Weekly Moving Average

Wogalter, Michael S., 73

Wyckoff, Richard D., 6

XHB. *See* homebuilders

XLU. *See* energy

XLV. *See* health care

XOP. *See* oil

XRT. *See* retail

Yellen, Janet, 76

yields, 178

ABOUT THE AUTHOR

I have an uncommon background that makes me uniquely qualified to write this book. Growing up, my parents never discussed finances beyond the copious complaints about how little money we had, how difficult it was for my dad to hold two jobs, and how I had better get cracking at making money, beginning with taking babysitting jobs when I was twelve.

My parents thought I should become a teacher. So I did. By the mid-1970s, I earned a master's degree in special education, married a boy from the neighborhood (Queens, New York), and tried my hand as a homemaker.

I left Queens and my first husband in 1977. With a job working as a special education teacher in a private school in Manhattan, teaching kids with significant emotional disabilities, I crossed the 59th Street Bridge to my first four-story walk-up studio apartment on West 84th Street and Riverside Drive and never looked back.

Eventually, I took a job working in the New York City Public Schools, staying with the same special education population. My annual salary of $9,000 was barely enough to make ends meet. But I was happy and independent!

In 1978, while I watched the New York Yankees play in the World Series, a knock on my door changed everything! A neighbor came by to invite me up to her apartment to watch the game with a few of her friends. My neighbor worked on the New York Commodities Exchange in the World Trade Center, as an analyst for Merrill Lynch. She took me under her wing and brought me down to see the Exchange. My eyes popped out, my heart raced, and the proverbial light bulb went on over my head. I knew at that moment, this was it. I had found my calling!

Through an admittedly circuitous route, I landed a job working for Paul Sarnoff at Conticommodity Services, Continental Grain's Futures Division. Mr. Sarnoff placed me on the Coffee, Sugar and Cocoa Exchange, talking on a squawk box to brokers throughout the world about the daily goings-on in all three of the commodity markets. Each afternoon, I wrote market commentary. My analysis was transmitted globally.

Considering that I began my auspicious career with zero knowledge and even less money, I made it my business to learn all that I could in the least amount of time possible. Studying chart patterns became my window into not only how charts reflected past price movements but also how well they could predict probable future price movement. It was my first foray into market phases. Within my first year as an analyst, I gained a solid reputation as an expert chartist. With the self-confidence and money in my pocket from my work as a highly regarded analyst, for the first time in my life, I opened a trading account.

After my first year on the trading floor, Conticommodity offered me a membership and the chance to execute trades for the firm on the Coffee, Sugar and Cocoa Exchange. I had made it to the big time as a broker! The other members of the Coffee, Sugar and Cocoa Exchange dubbed me "Rookie of the Year."

Eventually, I worked my way over to the New York Mercantile Exchange. I became an independent broker (one who trades for their own account) trading mostly crude oil. In total, I spent twelve years on the floor, eventually leaving to trade "upstairs." The lessons I learned on the trading floor remain my foundation for trading today.

Simultaneously, I met a woman who had a daughter with Down Syndrome, which led me into advocacy work. I became a passionate enforcer of the federal Individuals with Disabilities Education Act (IDEA). With the same appetite that I employed when approaching trading, I became an independent consultant primarily for middle and high schools to help teachers and related service providers write adaptions and accommodations so that kids with significant disabilities could access and participate in the general curriculum. How fortunate for me that I was able to pursue two of my passions—education and finance!

In 2004, I observed that gold and silver were awakening from a long Bearish Phase into a Recuperation Phase. That event reignited an active interest in trading commodities. Then, during the recession in 2008, I got the opportunity to work as the director of trading education and research at MarketGauge.com. The company, known mainly for creating "tools" to help traders literally gauge the market, needed someone to write a daily financial blog, give trade recommendations, use social media to share market analysis, and teach courses to the public. A perfect fit for me.

Hence, I transitioned back into trading full time, but with occasional work as an independent inclusion specialist in Santa Fe, New Mexico. I focused on market phases.

After the market's dismal performance in 2008, and by the spring of 2009, I advised people through social media and the growing MarketGauge subscriber base on how to profit from the transition from a Bearish to a Recuperation phase (when stock market prices began to go up after a prolonged move downward). I was well ahead of the crowd!